HANDY AS HIP POCKETS ON A HOG

The Colorful Language
of the American Southwest

Jim Evans
Christmas gift 1989
from Bruce, Dana
and Blake Schumacher

Also by Donald Chain Black
Spoonerisms, Sycophants, and Sops

HANDY AS HIP POCKETS ON A HOG

The Colorful Language of the American Southwest

Donald Chain Black

TAYLOR PUBLISHING COMPANY
Dallas, Texas

Book Designed by Deborah J. Jackson-Jones

Copyright © 1989 by Donald Chain Black

All rights reserved.

No part of this book may be reproduced in any form without written permission from the publisher.

Published by Taylor Publishing Company
　　　　　　1550 West Mockingbird Lane
　　　　　　Dallas, Texas 75235

Library of Congress Cataloging-in-Publication Data
Black, Donald Chain.
　　Handy as hip pockets on a hog / Donald Chain Black.
　　　p. cm.
　　Includes index.
　　ISBN 0-87833-682-6 : $8.95
　　1. English language — Provincialisms — Southwestern States — — Glossaries, vocabularies, etc. 2. Americanisms — Southwestern States. 3. Southwestern States — Miscellanea. I. Title.
PE2966.B58 1989
427'.976 — dc20　　　　　　　　　　　　　　　　　　89-30438
　　　　　　　　　　　　　　　　　　　　　　　　　　　CIP

Printed in the United States of America

10 9 8 7 6 5 4 3 2 1

*In fond memory of the
other Donald Chain*

PREFACE

The third or fourth year I taught the vocabulary and etymology course that led to the writing of *Spoonerisms, Sycophants, and Sops / A Celebration of Fascinating Facts About Words,* I began to throw in an occasional folk phrase or local color aphorism in which I had found unusually bright imagery or humor. Although members of the class represented a broad spectrum of ages and backgrounds, they all seemed delighted to learn that *Arkansas strawberries* aren't fruit and that neither *hog wrestling* nor *Hoover hogs* has anything to do with swine. They were amazed and incredulous to find that not everybody in this world knows what *harrikins* and *pope's noses* are, and they responded by bringing, in considerable number, their own linguistic gleanings from around the four-states area.

Situated in a remote northeast corner of Texas, Paris is a good place to listen to the folk language of the Southwest. Frontier lore has it that Blossom, a hamlet ten miles to the east, lies upon the line of demarcation where the Old South stops and the West begins. My father and grandfather were born there, and five generations of my family have lived within twenty miles of this place. Twenty years of medical practice in Paris provided me with samples of speech from every stratum of the local society, and my past and present friendships with men and women of markedly disparate ages have helped a lot. I think that rural communities lend themselves to interaction between the young and the old better than cities do. My outspoken racetrack friend Spencer Abbett agrees that we live in the country. He says that Paris is so far out in the boondocks that people's idea of a seven-course meal is *a six-pack and a chitlin creole* — a telling phrase indeed, for the first item suggests the West and the last both the Deep South and nearby Cajun Louisiana.

My sole criterion for including a phrase in this book was that I had heard it spoken. Although long dead, my father was the book's chief contributor. A man of little originality, he nevertheless had a good ear, a retentive mind, and a startlingly accurate knack for using a homely aphorism in just the right place. It is he to whom this book is dedicated. The several hundred other contributors, my friends and students, deserve no less credit.

Because these students and friends had so much fun trying to "dope out" the meanings behind folk phrases that were novel to them — and then to pick a definition from a proffered list — I have cast this book in the form of multiple-choice questions with answers immediately following. Try your hand, then, at these examples from the colorful language of the American Southwest.

CONTENTS

	Preface	vii
1	From *Calf Lick* to *Calf Rope*: Down on the Farm	1
2	From *I Mean to Shout!* to *Would I Lie to You?*: Exclamations and Rhetorical Questions	13
3	From *The Chic Sales* to *Hoover Dust*: There's a Name for It	21
4	From *Dancing in a Hog Trough* to *Sippin' a Little Hair of the Dog*: Of Hogs and Dogs	37
5	From *Gussied Up* to *Grass Widow*: Ladies and Otherwise	49
6	From *Saying Grace* to *Sanctification*: In Hushed Tones	63
7	From *Arkansas Strawberries* to *Fish-Flavored Ice Cream*: Cooking on the Front Burner	73
8	From *Bull Calves* to *Tar Brushes*: It's a Matter of Heredity	87
9	From *All Wool and a Yard Wide* to *The High Five*: It's a Matter of Character	97
10	From *A Barrel of Snakes* to *Scarce-Hipped Hogs*: Beasts Domestic and Otherwise	111
	Invitation	125
	Bibliography	127
	Index	129

1

FROM
CALF LICK
TO
CALF ROPE

DOWN ON THE FARM

Daddy used to say we lived so far out in the woods that we had to walk towards town to go squirrel hunting.

The speaker who sums up another man's social standing by saying *"He didn't come to town two on a mule"* reminds you that the individual in question

- was not accompanied on his arrival.
- is a relative stranger to country-bred things.
- is not unable to work well alone.
- is not without substance and influence.
- is not a man without polished manners.

Variants of this Southern adage seem to vary with the agricultural geography of the speaker, from the forests of Arkansas (*He didn't come to town on no load of wood*) to the Rio Grande Valley (*on no load of watermelons*) to East Texas (*on no load of turnips*) to the Appalachians (*He could make you jump a nine-rail fence*). Certainly all these connote one's considerable wealth and influence. My favorite Southwestern superlative for a man of substance is one who *has enough money to burn up a wet mule*.

It's time to put the chairs in the wagon is really a folksy Southwestern (and gentle) way of saying

- "You should move out of town."
- "I'm ready for a divorce."
- "Let's go home."
- "Put up or shut up."
- "I expect to hear the truth from you."

Those earlier Americans who attended a brush-arbor revival or a singin'-all-day-and-dinner-on-the-ground clean-up day at the community cemetery were obliged to bring their own chairs, and a call for their return to the buckboard signaled the time for departure.* Though wagons have gone the way of outdoor revivals, the phrase is still in use with this meaning. *Let's light a shuck* means the same thing, although the practice of illuminating one's way with a burning cornhusk has been at rest for three generations.

In East Texas the ***harrikin, lights,*** and ***pope's nose*** are all

- poker terms.
- gastronomic delicacies.
- nautical landmarks.
- terms of endearment.
- varieties of tobacco.

The appellation for the tidbit of meat at the base of a cooked chicken's back dates to the Restoration, when some anti-Catholic Englishman likened it pejoratively to that portion of the papal visage (Innocent XI). By the time Longfellow rhapsodized upon it (his "epicurean morsel"), the delicacy had become the *parson's nose,* though the name of no eponymous American cleric has been recorded.

---

*Coon hunters' humble preparation for departure has left a less delicate phrase with identical meaning: *time to piss on the fire and call in the dogs.*

The duck hunter with whom I grew up positively asserted, with no authority whatever, that the filmy *lights* we removed from inside the backs of birds were used by them to find their way back south for the winter. These edible entrails (lungs) were ostensibly called *lights* because of their consistency.

Did the word for the mysterious *harrikin* (chicken ribmeat) of Texas somehow stem from the French *haricot* (kidney bean), or perhaps from the fourteenth-century English ragout (haricot) made from such tasty morsels? All is speculative, but in a humble chicken's back is to be found ever so much more linguistic meat than I might have guessed.

Twelve acres of pregnant red hogs is the epitome of

- homeliness.
- beauty.
- greed.
- pandemonium.
- malodorousness.

Situated (in intensity if not in imagery) smack-dab between *pretty as a speckled pup under a red wagon* and *pretty as dollar cotton,* this phrase is used (with a slight variation) by Dick Syatt in his *Like We Say Back Home* as a superlative of value (Husband to wife: "Honey, I wouldn't trade you for *twelve acres of pregnant red hogs*") in which the speaker uses for his figure the loveliest sight he can imagine.

If you take the country out of **There's a family difference between the ox and the whiffletree,** the result is something like

- Employer and employee don't always seek the same ends.
- Children don't invariably grow up like their elders.
- Husbands and wives don't always see eye-to-eye.
- Man and beast often work against each other.

Perhaps his biblical resonances have accorded the ox his mixed roles in so many subsequent folk sayings; although the ox is St. Luke's symbol and no less than a second-order angel (a cherub) in Ezekiel, his Deuteronomic position as a dumb brute deserving sympathy is a little closer to his later literary image: "You must not muzzle an ox when it is treading out the corn" (i.e., don't deny a faithful worker an occasional gratuity). Sometimes cited simply for his remote position in a team: *I don't know him from Adam's off-ox** (I wouldn't recognize him if I saw him), the creature plays only a little more active part in the origins of the dog in a manger. A dog in a manger is a man likened to the spiteful canine of the fable who slept in the manger, denying the ox the hay that the dog himself could not eat.

From Noah Webster's 1802 retelling of another fable ("The Farmer, the Lawyer, and the Farmer's Ox") comes "It makes a difference whose ox is gored." Only a remnant of the moral remains in the vernacular of the Southwest: *You gored my ox* (you caused trouble).

---

* the animal farthest from the driver, distinguishing him from the near-ox

Sometimes the animal at the whiffletree (singletree, the crossbar to which the ox is harnessed) is a mule, or even a donkey, any or all of which is likened to the husband, who is not always in accord with his whiffletree wife.*

Lick that calf again! is in every way akin to

- *I hear you cluckin' but can't find your nest.*
- *You're squattin' when you ought to be squawkin'.*
- *You're pulling the wrong pig's ear.*
- *You did it wrong!*
- *Grease me.*

Currently the analogous folksy way to say, "I can't understand you; could you repeat that?" is *I can't tell which way you're coming from,* but the more modern comment lacks the colorful, bucolic imagery of *I hear you cluckin' but can't find your nest."* The less tentative *Lick that calf again!* means "You did it wrong; do it again," with the same implication of incompleteness as *You didn't give it no more'n a lick and a promise.*

Similarly born in the fowl yard but with an altogether different meaning is *You're squattin' when you ought to be squawkin'* (You've failed to speak your piece), and from the nearby stable comes *He was geein' when he shoulda been hawin',* of similar meaning. *Pulling the wrong pig's ear* is no less in error than *barking up the wrong tree,* and *"Grease me"* simply means "Pass the butter."

---

* Albeit when the wife runs away from a marriage, it's *she* who's said to have *jumped the traces.*

She's as common as hens' tracks pegs the subject as

- humble.
- down-to-earth.
- country bred.
- poor.
- vulgar.

When I was scolded as a child by my Mississippi-born mother for my off-color language (more often than some, I expect), I might have been told that my turn of speech was *vulgar*. But her most serious imprecation was a word she reserved for only the direst linguistic offense: "That's *common*."* I can hear her disgust yet. Neither she nor her own mother ever kept fowl, but I heard her use the above pejorative (along with *common as pigs' tracks*) as if these barnyard imprints were an everyday sight suitable as a simile for the hoi polloi.

The *south end of a northbound nanny goat* often figures in a Southwestern phrase for one's

- offensiveness.
- appearance.
- appetite.
- contempt.
- misfortune.

---

* The term *ordinary*, in the pejorative sense of common or vulgar, got itself westernized about 1800 into *ornery*: ill-tempered.

In *The Yearling,* Jody Baxter scandalizes his mother with a well-known Florida line he's picked up from their earthy neighbors, the Forresters: "I'm so hungry, my belly thinks my throat is cut." She might have been even more shocked with another slack-stomached phrase from just west of them, *I could wipe my mouth with my belly.* In the South one's appetite seems to take precedence over pride (*He doesn't care what you call him, as long as you call him to supper*), etiquette (*Fingers were made a'fore forks*), or discrimination (*I could eat the south end of a northbound nanny goat*).

 rumor ***known by the chickens under the porch*** is

- unreliable: It's repeated only by the stupid.
- reliable: It's repeated by those who overheard it themselves.
- clandestine: It's been kept very close to home.
- factual: Those who *keep their ears to the ground* know it.
- common knowledge: Everybody's heard it.

Chickens seem to have been very near the end of the line when nature passed out respectability; whether it's about their untutorable ignorance (*Useless as takin' a chicken to Sunday school*), their last-resort job (*I'd rather get under the porch and peck with the chickens*),* or their deceptive ap-

---

* Sometimes worse: *I'd rather get a tin bill and peck shit with the chickens.*

pendages (*Wings don't mean a chicken can fly*), folk sayings have lent little dignity to fowl. *Even the chickens under the porch know that* suggests a rumor's widest dispersal, known even to those who are always the last to hear anything.

Last winter was real cold in Texas, but we kept warm on *prairie coal and shinny*. The italicized phrase restated is

- cheap lignite and increased physical activity.
- dried cow dung and whiskey.
- green mesquite firewood and venison (from illegally stalked deer).
- dead brushwood and making whoopee.
- crushed cornstalks and foxfire.

Innovative Southwesterners have put the lowly cow patty to a surprisingly large number of uses. A strong drink (cow-pen tea) made of this material was long recommended in folk medicine — at least until the end of the nineteenth century — to bring out the rash of measles and as a vermifuge. Ground up and bagged, the stuff brings a startlingly high price as garden fertilizer. And no Texas-style holiday, from the Terlingua chili cookoff to a San Jacinto Day beer bust, would be complete without a cow-chip throwing contest. It burns (as *prairie coal**) at least as well as the fake fireplace log you buy at the grocer's, and no chopping is required. Of course *shinny* is just one more name for 'shine, moonshine, homemade whiskey.

---

* sometimes, at least in West Texas, *Throckmorton firewood*

The origin of hollering **Calf rope!** as a signal of surrender is very likely from

- the Bible.
- Charles I.
- the kitchen.
- the rodeo.
- the range.

I've always suspected that the reason I was never able to acquire a taste for beer was that as a very young boy I watched my father blow the foam from his Lone Star with the comment that it had a good head of *calf slobber* on it. But I've never been sure, because the same man likened this substance to pie meringue, and I've certainly never lost my inherited taste for that confection.

An occasional variant of *There's mor'n one way to break a hound from suckin' eggs* is *There's mor'n one way to dress a calf's head.* The latter is itself a variant from a time in history much antecedent to any printed vernacular of the Southwest, for the English Calves' Head Club of the late seventeenth century met yearly on the anniversary of Charles I's execution, dining upon calves' heads dressed in various ways to ridicule that fallen monarch and his friends. *Brewer's Dictionary of Phrase and Fable* says the society disbanded in 1735, but the maxim lives on.

The ghost of an even older calf phrase enjoys commoner currency; St. Luke's *fatted calf* may still be figuratively killed in preparation for an elaborate celebration, with exactly the same implications of *Let's put the big pot in the little one.*

The cowboys who rope calves from horseback in rodeo competitions carry a short length of light rope (the calf rope) for binding the animals' legs as soon as they are thrown to the ground. Certainly the figure of surrender comes from the moment the calf is wrestled down, but the roper cannot holler "calf rope" or anything else, for the calf rope is carried in his teeth for instant readiness. A horseman who ropes a calf on the range participates in no timed competition, carries his calf rope in his belt, and is presumably free to holler.

2

FROM
I MEAN TO SHOUT!
TO
WOULD I LIE TO YOU?

EXCLAMATIONS AND RHETORICAL QUESTIONS

A plain-spoken man, Daddy believed a man should lay his cards on the table: *"Put it down where the calves can get at it."*

I'm going to **clean your plow** means you're

- having your farm equipment washed.
- going to be bathed.
- about to be purged.
- going to be spanked.
- being sued for all you're worth.

This was the last folk phrase I wrote for this book, going back to add it after I had finished all the rest. I'm sure it was because I had repressed it, along with *tan your hide* and *wear you out*. Daddy's favorites, they invariably preceded one of his thorough spankings, usually administered either for pure obscenity or for some disagreeable observation I'd made (*talking out of school*, he would have said). His choice of correction was not very effective, I guess: my plow's still not very clean, as you are perhaps beginning to see.

An East Texan who's given a **fare-thee-well** is

- presented with a gift.
- complimented.
- chastised.
- bid good-bye.
- wined and dined.

Additionally used both as a noun without an article (*She gave him fare-thee-well*) and an adverb (*She fare-thee-well ate*

his lunch), this deceptive phrase is often as close to castigation as it is to chastisement. The unfortunate recipient of such invective has *had a strip torn from his hide, been read the riot act, caught Billy Blue Hill,* or *been told how the cow ate the cabbage.*

The Northeasterner's rhetorical **"Would I lie to you?"** has surfaced in the Southwest as

- *Does the day follow the night?*
- *Does the sun come up in the east?*
- *Is the Pope Catholic?*
- *Does Dolly Parton sleep on her back?*

In Lufkin folklorist Bob Bowman's *If I Tell you a Hen Dips Snuff . . . /What Texas Good Ol' Boys Mean When They Say What They Do,* the author's titular aphorism (he completes it with *you can look under her wing*) seems curiously fragmentary, for in my neck of the woods — less than two hundred miles from his — the phrase is invariably completed with *you can look under her wing for the can.* In either case the speaker is assuring his listener that he may be relied upon for the gospel truth. Variations extend from summer (*If I tell you a hen hauls cotton, you can hitch her up*) to winter (*If I say it's Christmas, you can hang up your stocking*) and from good times (*If I tell you there'll be a dance, you can bring your fiddle*) to bad (*If I tell you it's going to rain, you can set out the catch barrel*). Like so many similar epigrams, such common rhetorical questions often seem to find their origins on the farm: bovine (*Does a bull make*

beef?), porcine (*Does a pig love slop?**), and asinine (*Does a mule eat corn?*).

The day following the night belongs to Polonius and Shakespeare, the rising sun echoes Ecclesiastes, and the Pope's avowed Catholicity is but another catchphrase couched in the tongue of the eastern United States. The observation of Ms. Parton's sleeping habits is of course from Dan Jenkins's *Baja Oklahoma,* smack in the heart of the American Southwest.

He plays right behind third base tags the subject as one who

- plays (any game) inexpertly.
- doesn't plan well for the future.
- is a radical or reactionary.
- plies a modest trade.
- is emotionally unsound.

But a half step from the commoner *out in left field,* this expression seems to reverberate in the patois of a dozen trades in addition to baseball: carpentry (*He's half a bubble off plumb*), masonry (*He's two bricks shy of a load*), seamanship (*He's rowing with just one oar in the water*), construction (*His elevator don't go all the way to the top*), cotton baling (*He ain't wrapped up too tight*), mechanics (*His clutch*

---

* or, less delicately, *Is a pig's ass pork?*

is slippin'), haberdashery (*He doesn't have all his buttons*), horology (*He ain't wound up too tight*), poultry-dealing (*He's outta the second settin'*), education (*He's studying to be a half-wit and ain't gonna make it*), mortuary science (*He's dead and too dumb to fall over*), and dog training (*He don't know "c'mere" from "sic'im"*).

W*utzi, pee, cope,* and *là* are all Southwestern

- children's words for various body functions.
- nineteenth-century terms of endearment.
- calls to animals.
- exclamations equivalent to *Shame on you!*
- words of surprise.

To call in his livestock, the Southwestern farmer draws from a wide choice of words. Although *soo, pigpigPIG!* is the most common call to swine in my part of East Texas, University of Texas Professor Atwood has shown that *wutzie!* is more often used in Central Texas, just as *turkturkturKEE!* has traveled west to become *pee!* The same linguist lists *cope!* as a call to horses, though he comments that whistling and calling the animal's name seems to be the most popular. Soothing words from a milker to a restless cow range from *soo, cow!, saw!,* and *co, boss!* in the west to the Cajun French *là!* of southern Louisiana.

I *mean to shout* describes one's

- intention to preach.
- positive disavowal.
- emphatic agreement.
- admission of guilt.
- determination to be heard.

I mean to shout is unquestionably the parent of the ubiquitous Southern *I mean.* In the shorter phrase the strongly accented (and invariably two-syllabled) *mean* denotes the speaker's agreement more emphatically than *I can't fall out with that* but less certainly than *You can't beat that with a hickory switch.* The superlative for a follow-up affirmation is the sonorous *If I'm lyin' I'm dyin'.*

In the Southwest **He's in the house** tells you the subject is anywhere indoors *except* the

- plunder room.
- parlor room.
- front room.
- kitchen.
- den.

In his *Regional Vocabulary of Texas,* E. Bagby Atwood shows that usage of the term *plunder room* (for storage room) is most concentrated in German (Central) Texas,

the German *Plunder,* lumber, having likely replaced the common English *lumber room. Front room* and *parlor room* for living room are much in current use, and together with the den are well within the space between the *veranda* and *back galley* (front and back porches). A century ago the architect of any good-sized Southern house situated its kitchen in a separate outbuilding. Though this design feature is no longer in use, the phrase *in the house* still excludes the kitchen.

3

FROM *THE CHIC SALES* TO *HOOVER DUST*

THERE'S A NAME FOR IT

Daddy was fond of both misquotation and mixed metaphors: *"Give a dog a bad name,"* he would say, *"and he won't be worth pea turkey doo."*

These Arkansas replies are in answer to what question?

- *"If things was any better, I'd think they was lyin' to me."*
- *"Fine as frogs' hair."*
- *"Cookin' on the front burner."*
- *"Fat and sassy."*
- *"Tol'able."*
- *"Fair to middlin'."*
- *"I'd have to get better to die."*

These answers, graded from the first (meaning almost unbelievably well) to the last (very badly indeed) are all quite common replies to the ubiquitous *"Hidy, hi' you?"*

He'd wear a straw hat to a Christmas tree tells you immediately that the subject is

- stubborn and individualistic.
- hot-natured and weatherproof.
- rural and unsophisticated.
- retarded and withdrawn.
- hallucinatory.

A *Christmas tree* in this sense is the party itself, once the staple yuletide entertainment of Western small-town America but now linguistically associated only with humble backwoods types who seem to care as little for personal

comfort as they do for fashionable headwear. Such lads are *so country you can smell stove wood on their breath.* Paris rancher and retired veterinarian Don Riddle offers a pithy caveat to any prospective employer of a cowboy: "Never hire a hand who wears a straw hat or smokes Bull Durham: [He won't ever work much because] he's always either chasing his damned hat or rolling a smoke." On the positive side, Doctor Riddle describes his ideal employee:

>A heller and a fighter,
>A wild hoss rider,
>And a pretty good windmill man . . .

 ll but one of these expressions originate from a single game. Pick the eccentric expression.

- *Clear the topwaters!*
- *A jewelry store!*
- *Dallas to Fort Worth!*
- *Baby fingers!*
- *A faint heart never filled a flush.*

A big raise after an opening bet is sometimes accompanied by *Let's clear the topwaters* (i.e., get rid of those players who are hanging on with marginal hands), and the phrase has escaped far enough from the poker table to describe any bold gesture designed to eliminate the fainthearted. A poker player may declare his hand to be a *jewelry store* (a diamond flush), a *Dallas to Fort Worth* (three

tens, for the thirty miles separating those cities*), or even *a dead man's hand* (aces and eights, the infamous hand held by Wild Bill Hickok just before he was shot by Jack McCall in an 1876 Deadwood poker game).

Phrases from this most American of popular card games have studded the language of the Southwest for a hundred years. Sometimes usage has changed the original term: *not playing with a full deck* may once have been an accusation to a hold-out cardsharper, but now the description is for one whose degree of intelligence is less than optimum. But *a faint heart never filled a flush* still counsels the calculated risk, and *like playing a hand with your eyes shut* remains a simile for any perilous maneuver attempted in the dark.

Of course *Baby fingers!* is the eccentric phrase, an exclamation from one marble shooter to another, who claims his right to goad his opponent with one finger while he's aiming his taw.

In the Southwest a *blue-gummer* is a

- displaced Yankee.
- turpentine logger.
- police detective.
- dangerous Negro.
- native Cajun.

---

* A hand of three tens is also *thirty miles of railroad track.*

A curious bit of folklore (God knows from where) surrounds the occasional black person whose gums are blue rather than pink: his bite is said to be poisonous. Frederic Cassidy's *Dictionary of American Regional English* dates the earliest printed reference of this folk belief to 1908, but his contributors offer no hint of its derivation (only the notation that it's not very well known). Perhaps countering this derogatory appellation, black speakers in East Texas equate *a real blue-gummer* with someone quite different: an enviable person, a real straight shooter.

Bahmanishous would have qualified for the latter praiseworthy cognomen. The Clarksville, Texas, woman who told me the tale of Bahmanishous recalled her yardman's first words to her when she asked his name: "They call me Bahmanishous."

He worked once a week for them for almost thirty years, and three generations of their family called him Bahmanishous, at least one of them remembering that he had thought at the time that the man's name might have been a corruption of some biblical word.

Through the years Bahmanishous had always been paid in cash, until one Saturday afternoon the woman of the house found herself short and tried to write him a check. She did the best she could with the spelling of his name, but Bahmanishous refused her proffered check, saying, "That ain't my name. I'm J.P. Harris. They call me bah mah 'nishuls."

 woman said to be attending **the chic sales**

- has gone to purchase young fowl.
- has adopted a baby illegally.
- has been indiscreet with a younger man.
- has excused herself to powder her nose.
- only trades at the most exclusive shops.
- has gone shopping for her children.

Charles (Chic) Sale must have been pleasantly startled at the success of his 1929 *The Specialist,* a 27-page booklet about his carpenter friend Lem Putt who built only outhouses: two million copies of his book had been sold by 1956. Sale's tale takes the form of an after-dinner address delivered by the semiliterate but articulate Putt,* who (among other bits of homely advice on his trade) recommends placement of the outhouse just beyond the woodpile, so that the women who attend it might more efficiently keep the kitchen wood box well stocked.

If Chic Sale was surprised at his story's popularity, he may very well have been astonished at what followed, for his own name became a euphemism for the outdoor toilet and — at least in East Texas — for the indoor bathroom that succeeded it. Like the earlier eponymous Thomas Crapper (b. 1837), inventor of Crapper's Valveless Water Waste Preventer (the flush toilet), he may have been less than pleased to see his name aligned with other euphemisms like *the Miss Jones, the goat house, the dingbat, the little white house on the hill, the hoodlum house, the California house, the stick closet,* and the place where one goes to *pay his water bill.*

---

* self-styled "champion privy builder of Sagamon County"

There's a *yellow jacket in the outhouse* is an indirect way of saying

- There's trouble afoot.
- It's raining.
- His parents aren't of the same race.
- *Some*body is absent-minded.
- Spring is here again.

The discovery of stinging wasps at large in a tiny room where one is partially unclothed evidently presented enough of a threat to lend itself as a phrase for impending trouble. Although perhaps less ominous than *Somebody throwed a dead cat down the well,* the figure is as colorful as *He's plowin' up snakes, He's stirring the fire with a sword,* or *He's got an ox in the ditch.* Whether it's a *fly in the buttermilk,* a *hair in the butter,* or a *tit in the wringer,* all these phrases reflect the approaching peril of one *who fishes in troubled waters.*

The male counterpart to the woman who attended *the chic sales* is the man who goes to

- *bleed his lizard.*
- *ball the jack in his rod.*
- *drag his dobber in the dirt.*
- *shake the dew off the lily.*
- *dip his wick in the strange.*

In a resident physicians' call room at the University of Arkansas Medical Center one night in 1960, I took part in what might very well have been the least intellectual nomenclature conference in all of medical history. Ably assisted by two hoary urologists with remarkably keen ears and retentive memories, our group of seven onomastic pundits cheerfully compiled a list (I decline to reproduce it here) of sixty-seven folk names for male genitalia. After almost thirty years I still cannot fathom how such a thorough survey could have missed them, but somehow neither *lizard* nor *lily* appeared on our list!

If we didn't make no tomatoes that summer, we **hubbed it** all winter long borrows its imagery from

- riding on the rims (because of worn-out tires).
- shopping at a cut-rate clothing store called The Hub.
- a wagon wheel mired to its axles.
- a folk word variant of *hobbled*.
- the jobs they had to take in town.

Although *riding on the rims* might describe the plight of a car owner whose tires are *so thin that you can see the air in them,* the original metaphor is drawn from the metal rim of the wooden wagon wheel rather than the pneumatic tire. The family thus described is *so poor they couldn't buy hay for a nightmare.*

A real clothing store in Clarksville, Texas, The Hub borrowed the reputation of a hub as a central gathering place rather than a limit beyond which a wheel can sink no

deeper. However modest its merchandise was, I never heard a verb made of the habit of shopping there.

The observation of this pathetically poor truck farmer compares his family's slogging through poverty to the way a wagon wheel became buried "up to the hubs" in the sticky black mud of the Cotton Belt. *As poor as sawmill rats* (or maybe *as lizard-eating cats*), the family in bad-crop years can look forward to very little progress indeed.* Perhaps people enjoy the brevity and strength of the word *hub* like they do *hog;* the words have found their ways into hundreds of aphorisms. A Houston hyperbole for a deluge-class rainfall is *hub deep to a Ferris wheel.*

 one-armed paperhanger is the epitome of

- intractability.
- inefficiency.
- ineptitude.
- indolence.
- industry.

Superlatives for industry seem inexplicably to have settled upon cats (*busy as a cat in a tripe shop* and *busy as a cat coverin' it up*), dogs (*busier than a one-eyed dog in a smokehouse* and *busier than a dog on a June bug*), and amputees (*busy as a one-armed paperhanger* and *busy as a one-legged man at an ass-kickin' contest*).

---

* One eloquent Hunt County resident summed up his plight: *"I'm as broke as Lazarus, and* he *had a dog."*

You just pissed in my hip pocket means the moist man

- believes you've denigrated his well-to-do position.
- thinks you've somehow swindled him.
- ruefully admits being upstaged.
- says you've quashed his motion.
- complains that you've ruined his punch line.

It's the brightness of his imagery that atones for this swindled man's crudity — and makes his figure of speech so popular in far West Texas — just as the *crazy as a peach-orchard boar* calls up the lively picture of the drunken swine among the fermented fruit, or the pushing of a *wheelbarrow with rope handles* draws an accurate metaphor of futility. You can almost feel the humid soil of the simile *warm as worm dirt*.

My uncle Ross is a shade-tree mechanic to every South Texas ear means the avuncular auto repairman

- is as accomplished as Longfellow's smith.
- learned his trade from his father.
- is really only a casual observer.
- operates a fraudulent business.
- is self-taught.

The metaphor of the do-it-yourself tinker who has taught himself informally — working on his own car under the

shade of a tree, rather than in a machine shop — has been extended to other trades as well. The *shade-tree musician,* with which the callithumpian South Texas hills seem to be filled, describes the guitarist or banjo plucker who has figuratively learned to play by sitting alone beneath a shade tree and working until he got it right.

When *I went to hold Bill's hind leg, I seen he wadn't up to snuff, tricked out in his rump-sprung Sundays and nearly callin' for Earl.* The speaker describes a

- sympathetic bail bondsman with a drunk prisoner.
- discreet minister with a down-at-the-heels parishioner.
- hallucinatory hospital patient not yet recovered.
- shabby country wedding with a sick groom.
- half-hearted bill collector working on the weekend.

The speaker is figuratively about to hold his friend's hind leg in preparation for shackling him into his matrimonial traces, for he has come to the ceremony to serve as best man. Bill's shabby and sat-out suit only makes his appearance worse, for the groom is generally unwell (*not up to snuff*) and specifically nauseated (*callin' for Earl*). The *Earl* of the latter figure is onomatopoeic rather than eponymic, evidently in description of the victim's retching.

The man who **_wouldn't walk a mile to see a pissant eat a bale of hay_** has become the epitome of

- stupidity.
- laziness.
- worthlessness.
- indifference.
- incredulity.

In a land where _tilting at windmills_ has become _pissing into the wind_, it seems to be the hapless beast that is so often presented in similes for worthlessness: useless as a _crippled gelding_, a _wild ox fart_, or a _pinch of dried possum poop_. One ironically needs something about as much as a _fish needs a bicycle_, a _hen needs a toothbrush_, or a _pig needs a sidesaddle_. _Two carriages in a one-horse town_, _teats on a boar hog_, and a _grasshopper in a henhouse_ are of little more value than an _umbrella for a duck_, a _prayer book for a dog_, or _hip pockets on a hog_. All these are epitomized by the worthlessness of the incurious man who wouldn't walk a mile to witness the insect's gargantuan meal.

An apocryphal **_Cooter Brown_** has left his name as the epitome of

- drunkenness.
- corruption.
- avarice.
- sloth.
- lust.

Every age has sought superlatives among both man and beast for the direst degrees of inebriation. No less than the classical god of gods is still epitomized in East Texas for his bad habits (*drunk as Zeus*) as well as his good ones, and the mighty King Jeroboam I was well enough remembered for his tippling to have his name eponymously attached to the 4/5-gallon jug containing wine (*jeroboam*).* Geoffrey Chaucer chose rodents (*drunk as a mouse*), and poet Matthew Prior (d. 1721) looked no further than to his potted paramour for his simile (*drunk as Chloe*). Shakespeare's "One drunkard loves another of the name" is still heard in various forms.

Captain Francis Grose told a ribald story in his *1811 Dictionary of the Vulgar Tongue* about the drunken wife of David Lloyd, a Welch tavern keeper. Passing out in a pigsty proved her linguistic undoing, so that *drunk as David's sow* is now well into its second hundred years of currency.

Brewer's Dictionary of Phrase and Fable suggests that *drunk as blazes* may harken less to Hades than to the followers of St. Blaise (*blaiziers*) who drank to this patron saint of diseased creatures, both man and beast. Among Paul Dickson's heroic list of 2,231 words for drunkenness in his *Words* appear dozens of besotted beasts, including the probably innocent *coot,* and it may be that the shadowy *Cooter Brown* has somehow emanated from the infamous fowl. In any case it's Mr. Brown who has acquired the superlative: not just tipsy or tight or tippled, but knee-walking, Earl-calling, commode-hugging, fiddler's bitch†
— well, *drunker than Cooter Brown.*

---

* but not as mighty as the *nebuchadnezzar,* which holds twenty quarts

† The musician of yore received his wages in spirits, which he evidently both drank himself (*drunk as a fiddler*) and shared with his consort (*drunk as a fiddler's bitch*).

In the 1930s **Hoover hogs** were really

- jackrabbits.
- armadillos.
- coyotes.
- possums.
- raccoons.

Phrases containing proper names like this one, along with *Miz-Astor rich, I don't give a Rhett, Adam's off-ox, big Ike-ing around,* and maybe even *Fiddle britches and Tom Jones!* leave little doubt as to the identity of their eponymous donors, but I think that recognition is long overdue for the scores of forgotten people who have for decades lent their names to aphorisms, similes, and exclamations. Some of these surname-less bywords have clearly found their ways into the vernacular of the Southwest simply by their alliterativeness:

> *sorrier than Sadie*
> *stupid as Simon*
> *hotter'n Hannah's hairbrush*
> *bad as Ben's beans*
> *hung high as Haman*
> *out like Lottie's eye*
> *dull as Henry's old hoe*
> *crazy as a Bessie bug*

and another group through assonance:

> *O lawdy Aunt Maudie!*
> *Good golly Miss Polly!*
> *Lawdy, lawdy, Miss Claudie!*
> *Nina Ross rode a fartin' hoss!*

Even slant rhyme (*Don't that put Mel in jail!*), euphemism (*What in Sam Hill?*), and consonance (*Oh lawzy Miz Agnes!*) can be cited, but many phrases remain resistant to the pigeonhole. Surely some tall, beautiful Sara could emerge from history to claim *long-tall Sally,* an angry Catherine for *Katie bar the door,* a shamefaced Edward to admit to *ugly as Ned in the first reader,* and an industrious Jessica for *a goin' Jessie.* But I fear this commemoration may be the first and the last for the shadowy likes of Jacob and Benjamin of *He goes all around Jake's barn* (can't make his point) and *tough as Ben's shoe;* their possibilities for eventual linguistic recognition may be a little like *the last button on Gabe's coat.*

Although the unappetizing flesh of each of the animals mentioned was eaten by the economically distressed Southwesterners of the thirties, the humble armadillo got the name of the Depression president. In Roy Wilder, Jr.'s *You All Spoken Here,* he explains how the same hard times among his fellow North Carolinians produced *Hoover dust* as well, when out-of-work smokers would crumble discarded tobacco leaves for their roll-your-own cigarettes. In addition to the well-known *Hoovervilles* and *Hooverizing,* ole Herbert left the reversible *Hoover apron* for the cook and the *Hooverette* for the frugal housewife, a loose-fitting smock to be worn over her clothes.

4

FROM
DANCING IN A HOG TROUGH
TO
SIPPIN' A LITTLE HAIR OF THE DOG

OF HOGS AND DOGS

He said the only thing in this world that could be *happier than a hog in slop* was *a dog with two tails.*

When Sara Lee stepped off the carpet, Jackie had to dance in the hog trough. From this statement the alert folklorist knows that the two women are sisters and that

- Sara Lee inherited everything and Jackie got nothing.
- Sara Lee got pregnant by Jackie's boyfriend.
- when Sara Lee had her monthlies, Jackie had to do the chores.
- Jackie is older than Sara Lee.
- Sara Lee is older than Jackie.

The *Dictionary of Americanisms* places the date 1888 on the phrase *out on the carpet* (eligible for marriage, looking for a husband) but does not explain the imagery. Is the woman with matrimony on her mind figuratively on the carpet of her parlor room, entertaining suitors? Or has she perhaps rolled out the red carpet for a hopeful swain who is *carrying straws* to her ("sparking")? Nothing is clear except that the inversion, *stepped off the carpet,* means that Sara Lee has married.

The curious activity of *dancing in a hog trough** is what it is said a woman must do if her younger sister marries first. Whether the phrase is to be equated with other figurative, futile activities such a *barking at the moon* and *whistling Dixie,* or whether it suggests that the vanquished one must do her dancing in a narrowly circumscribed place is unclear. The social indignity of such an event has always been more pronounced in the East than in the West, and

---

* sometimes *dancing in the half-peck*

having one's younger sibling marry first is indeed still a matter of some shame in many Asian countries.

Calling one *on the carpet* found its origin in the church ceremony in which the miscreant is tried (and sometimes convicted and sentenced in open church) on the carpet in front of the pulpit.

One who is **calling his hogs** but who is not at an Arkansas Razorback game is most certainly

- about to marry.
- pregnant.
- nauseated.
- misbehaving.
- asleep.
- dead.

The liturgical churches' practice of proclaiming an approaching wedding among its members (publishing the banns) has traveled to the West as *being called out in meeting*. An appropriate subsequent experience for a bride so called out might be to find herself *called to straw* (pregnant), a condition that might very well lead to nausea (*calling for Earl*). Of less significance is being *called down* (reprimanded for misbehavior); of much more is being *called home* (dying).

One who *calls his hogs* but is not a football fan is snoring, *sawing logs, calling his cows, hitting the knots,* or *calling his pigs to market.*

***W**hen it gets right down to the lick-log,* they'll elect a Republican. The italicized phrase could be replaced without change of meaning by

- *When it gets down to the nitty-gritty* . . .
- *When it gets down to the nut-cuttin'* . . .
- *When the chips are down* . . .
- *When push comes to shove* . . .

Each of the three women in my life — mother, wife, and daughter — has been in turn dismayed when I've pointed out to her (discreetly, but not without relish) the origin of the word she's just used; *nitty-gritty** is a little like *jazz*: if everybody knew its origin, you might not hear it spoken as often.

The second alternative above comes from the ranch operation in which steers are made from bulls, and the third is worn but still warm from the poker table. Both suggest ultimate moments often expressed as taking place "in the eleventh hour" (the speaker or writer of such chronology invariably means *twelfth hour*, though every listener or reader understands he's being told of something happening in the last hour). Impending violence is implied in *When push comes to shove,* just as it is in its twin brother, *When stoop comes to grunt.*

To supply his cattle with essential salt, the early American stockman improvised a trough from a hollowed log. This *lick-log,* often placed near a hayrack, found its way into the vernacular of a famous Southwestern hero who was well known for his colorful turn of phrase. In *A Dictionary of Americanisms,* editor Mitford Mathews suggests a con-

---

* Black English for the innermost portion of the vagina

nection between David Crockett's "I was determined to *stand up to my lick-log, salt or no salt*" and his "I was determined to *stand up to my rack, fodder or no fodder.*"* It is very likely that Crockett's dutiful expression for facing up to an unwelcome task fathered the later phrase designating an emergent situation.

Y*ou can't hardly slop sprinklers and dippers at the same trough* is a bucolic observation on the

- preferences of tobacco users.
- reticences of amateur scholars.
- incompatibilities of astrological signs.
- differences of religious believers.
- disaccord of the old and the young.

Perhaps because they seem trivial, the doctrinal differences between the baptismal sacraments of the Methodists (sprinklers) and the Baptists (dippers) have borne the burden of many a soggy anecdote, but through them all the former continue to asperge† and the latter to immerse. Bible-belt fundamentalists still occasionally conduct these rites in creeks and stock-watering tanks, at least when weather permits, and they would be more than a little ill at ease with the other sect if they were to try to work out their differences, at a meal or elsewhere.

---

* both from *A Narrative of the Life of David Crockett,* Philadelphia, 1834

† "Get much rain at your place last week?" "Naw, no mor'n *a Methodist shower.*"

T he man who's just spent an evening at **hog wrestlin'** has been

- competing in a rodeo.
- shooting heroin.
- dancing with ugly women.
- driving his team through the mud.
- eating chitlins.

Perhaps the first really humanitarian conviction of my childhood came to me when I was told how on one night each month my father and his friends went to cook chitlins in the kitchen of the county jail. No wife would permit such a thing in her house, and though it was forty years ago, I remember the noisome smell of boiling and frying hog intestines as if it were yesterday. That these men subjected the locked-up and helpless prisoners to this culinary stench brought the inmates of the jail more sympathy from me than they probably deserved.

But my father and his friends weren't wrestling with hogs or any part of them; that's the phrase for the fate of any man who's been obliged to dance with an unattractive woman. He may even have had a partner whose unfortunate appearance requires her *to sneak up on a mirror,* one who looks like *she's been beat with an ugly stick,* or even one who *could haunt a house for fifteen cents.**

---

* or worst of all: *so ugly she could cook naked for a deer camp.*

 blind hog figures as the epitome of

- ineptitude.
- worthlessness.
- helplessness.
- fatigue.
- humility.

Various expressions for worthlessness (*about as useful as two buggies in a one-horse town*), helplessness (*He couldn't pound sand in a rat hole*), fatigue (*I feel like I been rode hard and put up wet*), and humility (*lower'n a mole's navel on digging day*) curiously omit the all-purpose hog, who so often figures in such metaphors and similes. Maxims for ineptitude range, as usual, from the bestial to the obscene. *A man who could screw up a two-car funeral* or *tear up a crowbar* is worse off than one who *couldn't hit a bull in the ass with a bass fiddle* but not as inept as one who *couldn't get a prostitute a date on a troop train* or even one who *couldn't organize a piss-off in a brewery*.

This sort of unfortunate bumbler is unable to perform even simple tasks that are *no hill for a climber* or *not much for a high stepper* and can only assuage himself with the hopeful sentiment that *any mule's tail can catch cockleburs* and that, now and again, even *a blind hog'll find an acorn*.

The hair of the dog is good for the bite

- is illustrated by the ancient tale of Mithridates.
- is the underlying principle of homeopathy.
- echoes an ancient treatment for hydrophobia.
- describes a medically sound remedy for a hangover.

The king of Pontus (first century BC) foiled his would-be poisoners with his long-term strategy of consuming minute portions of all the known poisons of his time, thus immunizing himself against their toxic potions. Consciously or otherwise, Mithridates followed the ancient dictum of homeopathic medicine, *similia similibus curántur* (like things cure like ailments). Later medieval practitioners utilized this same principle, treating the victims of hydrophobia by administering some tissue (usually hair) from the rabid animal that had bitten them. That this remedy never worked may have led to the alternate and opposite *allopathy (contraria contraries curántur)*, advocating the icing down of fevers and the purging of those with appendicitis (equally ineffective).

Modern gastroenterologists have admitted, not without chagrin, that small doses of alcohol do indeed allay the nausea of those who suffer from alcoholic overindulgence: rather an irony, that two thousand years of fatal medical experimentations were required to find a valid illustration for this usually futile therapeutic theory that has found its way into the American vernacular.

S_he was vaccinated with a Victrola needle_ tells you that she

- sings very well indeed.
- has a tin ear.
- was born to a musical family.
- is irretrievably stagestruck.
- is tiresomely verbose.

Rationality (which is not always operative in the design of folk metaphors)* would seem to dictate the subject's immunity to things musical (has *a tin ear*), at least it would be so if the speaker's figure followed Jenner's principle of vaccination. She might under other circumstances be as musical as the baby who *cuts her teeth* on a band director's baton, but this is once again too rational, for her tunes are only *chin music*. It's the mechanical and continuous features of the phonograph that make the metaphor; the lady is tiresomely talkative. Her tongue is *tied in the middle and flapping at both ends,* and she has *enough tongue for six rows of teeth.* She could talk

- *the legs off a stove.*
- *the gate off its hinges.*
- *the horns off a billy goat.*
- *the wings off a chicken.*
- *the cow out of her calf.*
- *the coon out of the tree.*
- *the balls off a brass monkey.*
- *the pump into believin' it's the windmill.*

---

* Tom Lehrer said the reason folk songs are so awful is that they are written by the folks, and I think his dictum is often true of folk sayings as well.

The condition of the ***town dog*** is the apogee of

- obesity.
- meanness.
- poverty.
- hopelessness.
- modesty.
- terror.

It's the *junkyard dog* whose bad temper is legendary, although it is likely that his original meanness was due to poverty rather than the kind of orneriness one expects from a *snappin' sow* or *a government mule*. It's the *cut dog** who has no chance, the *modest dog* who gets little meat, and the *scalded dog* who's been scared out of his wits.

In the halcyon days of my childhood in Red River County, Texas, an owner of one of the stores around the square would as a matter of course bring his dog to work with him each day. Such a dog had the run of the town, knew everybody, and was fed by just about all the regulars. The consequences of his high living cast his lot as the epitome of those who overindulge, *fat as a town dog*.

*i.e., castrated

Since the nineteenth century, and possibly as far back as the eighteenth century, every young woman who was *out on the carpet* employed *beau-catchers*, her word for

- telephones.
- breast pads.
- curling irons.
- love letters.
- French lace.

Every budding vamp counted the telephone in her armamentarium, but she called it *an Ameche* after 1939, that being the year of *The Story of Alexander Graham Bell*, a movie starring you-know-who. Her more intimate equipment might include a padded brassiere, but she termed that a *gay deceiver* and until recent years kept the word *falsie* general enough to include padding at any body site that needed augmentation. Reserved for her love letters was the evocative French *billets-doux,* sweet notes. *French lace* has to do with neither things Gallic nor tatted; it's just brandy, the sort with which one might lace her coffee or tea.

Beau-catchers followed *curling irons* and preceded *curling tongs,* the last of which has become simply *curlers.*

5

FROM *GUSSIED UP* TO *GRASS WIDOW*

LADIES AND OTHERWISE

Daddy liked to tell about the rube who was *so country he thought* poontang *was a town in Vietnam.*

They treated her like she was wearing a fidity bag means the woman was

- accorded the deference due a woman of substance.
- thought to be a witch who could cast a spell.
- engaged to another and unavailable.
- in mourning.
- avoided.

The use of asafetida lingered in folk medicine long after it was abandoned by practitioners in the last century. This foul-smelling substance (ground fennel root, where I come from) was worn in a little cloth bag hung about the neck, ostensibly to ward off contagious disease. Detractors joked that it was often effective, but only because the wearer smelled so bad that he was avoided by both the well and the sick. In *Penrod Jashber,* a reminiscent novel about his childhood, Booth Tarkington described the painful experiences of a boy who was forced by his overzealous parents to wear an "asafid'ty" bag around his neck.

When I did my postgraduate medical training at the University of Arkansas Medical Center at Little Rock, I saw many infants and children of the Ozark hill people who had received this folk remedy, either by mouth or on their skins. A friend of mine who was a medical investigator there suspected that asafetida might be poisonous, and in the liberal spirit of the sixties he acquired a government grant and set out to demonstrate his suspicions. Charlie administered ever-increasing doses of asafetida to two generations of laboratory rats, but he never killed a one. The stuff must expend all its potency emanating its awful odor.

The best asafetida story I ever heard is from Jim Hickman of Paris, Texas, where fifty years ago the crusty and outspoken town pharmacist received a request from Austin Hefflefinger for a nickel's worth of asafetida. When the customer asked whether he could charge it to his account, the testy druggist said, "Hell no, you can't. I'm not going to write 'Hefflefinger' and 'asafetida' for a nickel's worth of *anything!*"

She found a mare's nest when she jumped the broom describes the subject's

- impetuosity.
- schizophrenia.
- terror.
- disillusionment.
- fulfillment.

In the far reaches of my enfeebled memory lurks the image of some sort of folk ceremony in which a bride or a newly married couple steps or dances over a broomstick, but I can find a written description nowhere. The interesting contrast between the new and the old is clearer; to *jump the broom* is an East Texas phrase meaning simply "to marry," while *Brewer's Dictionary of Phrase and Fable* records the older *to jump over the broomstick* or *jump the besom* as descriptions of a common-law marriage only, a union without ceremony. This feature is in no way implied in the Texas phrase currently in use (along with the commoner *tie the knot* and the commonest *get hitched,* the last harkening back to the ox and the whiffletree).

Whether the subject's nuptials were with or without ceremony is in this case immaterial, for her marital experience was disillusioning; she found less than she had anticipated. Mares make no nests, just as hens cut no teeth and horses grow no feathers. Her expectations of wedded bliss were reduced to nonsense, *moonshine,* * *mares' nests,* and *horsefeathers,* as rare and as unnatural a thing as *hens' teeth.*

Spread out like a cold supper describes a woman's

- generosity.
- meanness.
- sexuality.
- household.
- corpulence.

Folk sayings about obesity aren't uniformly disparaging: *Fitter than a fat lady* denotes something or somebody in good condition; *fat, dumb, and happy* is the picture of satisfaction; and one who says he's *come to town just to see the fat lady sing* is simply asserting his attentiveness. But my father often characterized the cold supper lady as one who *couldn't sit down in a number-three tub,* one whose derriere measured *two ax handles wide.* Overfed as *the town dog,* the subject *didn't have no sideways; when somebody hollered "Haul ass!" she had to make two trips.*

---

* If you've ever drunk any *moonshine* or *white lightnin'* (strong homemade whiskey), you'll probably agree that the same word serves well for *nonsense,* just as do the British *shandygaff* (beer and lemonade) and *balderdash* (beer and buttermilk).

She don't sweat much, for a fat gal (said of a slender woman) may be accurately translated as

- She's guilelessly pretending to be something she's not.
- She's a cool and clever liar.
- I can find little good to say about her.
- Hard times have made her fall off right smart (i.e., lose a lot of weight).
- She doesn't feel much guilt, for a complacent sinner.

Far from crude, this folk saying is a tactful expression of one's inability to find *anything* attractive about the woman: The speaker's fumbling about for a tacit disclaimer of his conviction exemplifies his country-bred but gentle manners.

I saw her at the wedding reception, and she was all *gussied* up. The italicized word is

- an eponym from *Gussie,* Augusta.
- from the dressmaker's *gusset,* gore.
- from the French *gousset,* armpit.

Brewer suggests that *dressed up to the nines* might be a corruption of *to then eyne* (to the eyes), implying head-to-toe arrayal in one's very best bib and tucker (lace shawl). South Louisiana superlatives first shortened *all gussied*

up* to *all got up* and then to an even shorter adjective, as for a fancy shirt, a *got-up* shirt.

Whether some eponymous Augusta was responsible for being the first described in such finery is not altogether clear, and the triangular *gusset* (from Old French *gousset*, armpit, where a piece of armor like a pod, *gousse*, once fit) or gore sewn into a dress is put there more often for reinforcement or enlargement than for decoration. For the latter reason, I prefer some archetypal, got-up Gussie as a source, but nobody really seems to know for sure.

H *is wife had to sit on a sack of fertilizer to raise her umbrella* describes

- her stature.
- his farmland.
- her looks.
- his poverty.
- a thunderstorm.

My favorite horse-racing companion, who will *poor-mouth* anybody who'll listen to him — and to whom the definition of personal wealth begins with anybody who smokes *ready-rolls* — explains his persistent presence at

---

* The Southwesterner is no less likely than any other American to make verbs of everything, ranging from casual acquaintances (*We've howdied but ain't shook*) to unruly horses (*He's broke but needs to be gentled*) to uncooled coffee (*It's been saucered but ain't been blowed*).

the two-dollar window by saying simply, *"Poor folks have poor ways."* This same wag is inordinately fond of superlatives for the sorriness of things in general (*sorrier than gully dirt, sorrier than bar-ditch hay*) and land in particular. Like the poor farmer's wife who has difficulty with her umbrella, most of his metaphors play upon the ambiguous meaning of *raise*: Their land was *so sorry you can't raise your voice on it, so sorry two red-haired women couldn't raise a fuss on it,* or *so sorry they had to shovel cow manure under the pole before they could raise the flag.*

One man's comment to another about a mutual acquaintance, **He took up with a grass widow and a wood's colt,** might for some ears require further explanation:

- He has in his barn both a brood mare and a yearling.
- He has both a home-loving wife and a torrid lover.
- He collected his debts ruthlessly and violently.
- He found a new home and a ready-made family.
- He's contracted a venereal disease.

The vernacular of the Southwest, as that of other cultures and other generations, has sought alternatives for the ungentle word *bastard*. While misuse of the adjective *illegitimate* (as a noun) is far and away the most common euphemism, more colorful designations for the *sidehill*

child or *sooner baby* range from the *outside child* of Black English to the *passion child* of the hippy. One form of the *child born on the wrong side of the blanket* takes an equine origin from the name for an offspring of the strayed mare and her unknown mate: the *wood's colt*.

Perhaps a similar (but more obscure) pastoral figure gave rise to the renaming of a divorcee as the *grass widow** with whom the mutual acquaintance has gone to live (*taken up with*).

ll she has to her name is a Butterick pattern dress tells you she's

- a clever seamstress.
- straightforward.
- unfashionable.
- impecunious.
- unassuming.

Among the many class lines drawn in the western America of thirty or more years ago was the sartorial division between those who were obliged to sew their own clothing and those who were not. While the advent of inexpensive ready-to-wear clothing has limited this distinction, the phrase for the impoverished one who owns nothing but such a humble garment has been broadened to describe the state of any poor woman, a sad companion for the man who's *broke as a stick horse*.

---

* as distinct from *sod widow*, a woman widowed by death

Like a *missum* describes

- an effeminate man.
- a thin slice of cheese.
- a poor marksman.
- a near-fatal illness.
- a surface-to-air rocket.

In the little Texas town where I grew up, the butcher was so careful with his cuts that anything from an implausible tale to a worn-out tire could be characterized as *thin as Floyd Ables' baloney*. *Missum* is created from the verb (in this case when the carver's knife very nearly misses the block of cheese) that makes the niggardly slice.

She *threw her hat over the windmill* suggests that the subject

- decided to run for public office.
- took on a formidable adversary.
- hatched out a fanciful idea.
- took leave of her senses.
- relinquished propriety.

The key to the origin of this provocative Southwestern adage turned up in the fortuitous discovery of the identical figure in French idiom, *femme qui a jeté son bonnet pardessus les moulins*. It's as if the flinging of the hat were an

appropriate gesture before she *let down her hair,* for she has thus said her farewells to propriety.

The Parisian windmills (*moulins*) of the 1870s that were converted into nightclub-brothels and made artistically famous by Toulouse-Lautrec's Moulin Rouge sketches and Renoir's *Moulin de la Galette* possessed just the sort of ambience needed to provide a setting for a woman bent upon indiscreet behavior. The phrase has weathered its transatlantic crossing and its hundred years' use very well: its tone and meaning remain the same.

Now, *it takes a mighty big woman to weigh a ton* is synonymous with which of the following:

- Aren't you stretching the truth a little?
- Be careful of what you're saying.
- I need evidence to believe what you've told me.
- Exaggeration is next door to lying.

My father's usual admonition and remonstrance to me for telling a fib was the shorter, "Now, son, the Lord's everywhere," but I'd heard him refer to the weighty woman with exactly the same meaning. Although any of the four proposed answers might fit this observation under the right circumstances, any correct substitution must convey only mild skepticism. Outright (if not outraged) incredulity finds its voice in the yet-more-dubious *Talk is cheap, but it takes real money to buy whiskey,* reserved for the liar who's so egregious that *he has to have his wife call the dog.*

Modern domestic technology has advanced *That about puts the rag on the bush* to which of the following?

- It beats all I ever saw!
- That sums it up.
- That'll wrap it up.
- That's the last straw!
- That puts it in the can.

The homemaker of two generations ago spent her Mondays with a paddle over a wash pot, a scrubbing board over a number-two tub, and a hand-wringer over a clothes basket. The welcome last step of her onerous chore was hanging out the washing to dry. The shirts and dresses filled the clotheslines, and lesser garments were spread on whatever stretches of *bob war* (barbed wire) fence were handy. The last humble cup towels and dishrags were relegated to the least reliable drying places available, the bushes that grew around the wash bench. It was the finality of the last act (as implied in all choices but the first) that earned it its last-straw significance, in much the same way as *That about puts the lid on the jar* has descended from the last step in the once common process of home canning.

Don't that take the rag off the bush! is similar to the exclamation offered as the first choice, an expression of incredulity or amazement — originally, that any thief could be petty enough to steal such a humble item. *She's taken the rag off the bush* means she's engaged, although the imagery for this last figure of speech is far from clear. One contributor to Mitford M. Mathews' *A Dictionary of Americanisms* suggested that this sort of rag referred to the one riflemen used for target practice, and that the phrase arose from the available woman's having been figuratively "picked off" by her sharpshooter husband-to-be.

How would you rather be described?

- *a real floozie*
- *a real doozie*
- *a real Christmas goose*
- *a real Uncle Deal*
- *really givey*

Every source I have lists the origin of *floozie* as unknown, but the possibilities are tantalizing. Always defined as not just a prostitute but a *cheap* prostitute, *floozie* could very well have been derived from a small coin of India, the *floose* (it's in the *Oxford English Dictionary*, honest Injun). That a variant is spelled *faloosie* leads toward the ever-risqué French with their *phalleuse,* raising numerous other lily-like possibilities. In any case most people wouldn't relish being so described.

Despite its apparent connotations of holiday merrymaking, *wilder than a Christmas goose** suggests a woman whose morals are little better than the floozie's and is thus another unwholesome term.

Uncle Deal is just one more of those uncommemorated, eponymous donors whose complete name has been linguistically lost: *lazy as Uncle Deal* denotes somebody hardly worth shooting. *Givey* suggests nothing philanthropic; it's only a term for someone weak or perhaps drunk, rubbery legged.

---

* only a step below the superlative *hog wild,* from the swine (*woods' hogs*) turned loose to fatten themselves on acorns and consequently quite intransigent beasts

Only *doozie* remains. The Deusenburg automobile once represented the quintessential luxury, the apogee of high living, so that anything — man or metal — akin to it must be a posh item indeed, one with which almost anybody would welcome association.

6

FROM SAYING GRACE TO SANCTIFICATION

IN HUSHED TONES

Daddy played enough poker in his time to say *"Church is out"* more than once.

A man who *sits on the back row and sings bass* is one who's

- communicative and gregarious.
- retiring and shy.
- discreet and closemouthed.
- religious and musical.
- faithful and genuine.

Along with being the appropriate position for bass singers in the church choir, the back-row seat designates the unassertive and unobtrusive spot for the *flâneur* rather than for the mover and shaker. But when the seat is filled by one whose voice augments the sound of the chorus but is seldom identifiable, the image emerges of the man who keeps his own counsel.

I*'ve got mor'n I can say grace over* expresses the speaker's

- attitude about her busy schedule.
- gratitude to a bountiful nature.
- ignorance of appropriate spirituality.
- acknowledgment of her undeserved good fortune.
- intemperate eating habits.

The attitude of this speaker — although she seems to imply that her cup runneth over — is rueful rather than religious, for she has just declined an invitation because of

her overfilled working schedule. She's *meetin' herself coming back from where she's been at.* Her farm-wife mother might have drawn her metaphor from more specific duties (*I've got to kill a chicken and churn*), from her flock itself (*I've got dirt to scratch and eggs to lay*), or even from a more recreational enterprise (*I'm catching 'em faster'n I can string 'em*), but all these mean precisely the same thing: "I'm too busy."

The Aggie who gets a **Baptist pallet in the parlor room**

- joins the church in a fashionable home ceremony.
- enjoys the most discreet accommodation in a brothel.
- attempts an unsuccessful seduction during a formal call.
- is given an unexpectedly warm reception by his girl friend.
- is evidently a late and superfluous guest.

Quips at the expense of the South's largest church, usually about its traditionalism (*hard-shell, foot-washin' Baptists*), its ubiquity (*The Baptists and the Johnson grass are takin' the country*), its conservatism (*Baptist preachers are so narrow they can sleep six to a bed*), or even its hypocrisy about abstention (*Where there's four Baptists, there's usually a fifth*)* are most often told by members of that denomination themselves. This is in contradistinction to Aggie

---

* A notable difference between Methodists and Baptists is that the former speak to each other when they meet in a liquor store and the latter don't.

jokes, which are seldom related by alumni of the Texas Agricultural and Mechanical University, an institution that long ago surpassed its pastoral image. I was personally present at what was later said to have been the official naming of the genre, when Cactus Pryor applied the name Aggie joke to a one-liner* he told at the Austin Civic Theater in 1953.

But the story of the luckless Aggie who slept in the parlor room (living room) had to do with neither the Baptist church nor romantic trysts; as an unexpected and superfluous guest, he had to sleep on the floor (a *Baptist pallet*).

He was in tall cotton, but he got took down tells you the subject was

- rich but humbled.
- once prosperous but now straitened.
- mortgaged to the hilt and then foreclosed upon.
- well-to-do but religious.
- once articulate but now dumb.

The chief money crop of the South has understandably sprouted metaphors and phrases meaning everything from moneyed to meanest. *Pretty as dollar cotton* serves as a

---

* about the Aggie who was so dumb he thought Spade Cooley was a castrated Chinaman

superlative for pulchritude, beauty that any man would *cotton to,* while *She's so ugly she'd kill waist-high cotton* covers the other extreme of beauty, or rather the lack of it. *In tall cotton* or *pissin' in high cotton* describes one who's *sitting in the catbird seat,* and nonstop speech is characterized by *talkin' like a cotton gin in packing time. He had a hard row to hoe* pictures the sort of hardship that could lead to the figure for ultimate downfall: *His cotton didn't come up* (he failed).

He got took down means the subject became a born-again Christian, *got religion,* was "saved." His going down is probably in description of his heeding the minister's end-of-sermon call for new members, in response to which he rose from his pew and went down to the front of the sanctuary. The implication is that the spirit of the occasion *took him down.*

It rose like the prayers of the sanctified describes

- bread dough from the pan.
- a phoenix from the ashes.
- the aroma of soul food.
- a crocus from the snow.
- smoke from a barbecue grill.

I heard this first from the aunt of an old friend, whose impious but evocative simile described her jealous and rueful admission of the superiority of her mother-in-law's homemade bread. In fact her comparison was so apt and so vivid that the luscious loaves came to be called the prayers of the sanctified.

The couple who *eats supper before they say grace* are

- obese.
- indiscreet.
- irreligious.
- absentminded.
- famished.

In addition to sharing the rest of America's euphemisms for *pregnant*, like *in a family way*, *enceinte*, and *expecting*, Southwesterners have evolved a set of their own. Metaphors range from domestic (*She's bakin' a cake in her oven* and *She's knitting booties*), agricultural (*She's a heavy springer* and *She's coming fresh*), and orthopedic — unexplainably — (*She's broke her knee/leg/ankle*), to metaphysical (*She's storked* and *She's been stung by a serpent*) and horticultural (*She's swallered a watermelon seed* and *They planted their crop before they built a fence*).

Church is out is a figure of speech that a Southwesterner might say

- when his son brings home four *F*'s and a *D*.
- when he lays down his straight flush.
- when he's told the election was rigged.
- after the doxology is sung.

At the little college where I teach, last year's prize for positive thinking went to the basketball coach whose star

forward showed him his four *F*'s and a *D* and was told, "Son, you're concentratin' too much on one subject."

The coach might very well (albeit less positively) have said *"Church is out"* to mean the player's season was over. *Turn in your uniform* might follow, just as the poker player's *Read 'em and weep* might succeed his identical comment, as would *They're goners* finish up the comment on the corrupt politicians. Unlike Huck Finn, to whom this metaphor was the epitome of feeling good, most who say this signify finality: *that's that, put the chairs in the wagon, that's all she wrote.** Only after the doxology is the sentence inappropriate, at least metaphorically.

He *found himself moseying along between hay and grass* suggests the subject is

- still childish.
- in imminent danger.
- casually intrusive.
- idly loafing.
- steadily industrious.

In a *Texas Highways* article, etymologist Mary Helen Dohan writes that *mosey* came from the Spanish *vamos* ("let's go") by way of *vamoose*. This seems to me a linguistically lengthy journey, especially for a verb that more

---

* This last expression comes from the so-called "Dear John" letter. Consider the finality of this missive: *Dear John: I brung your saddle home* (i.e., found another lover).

often connotes deliberation than speed: in the Southwest *to mosey* most often suggests to saunter or to loiter. In keeping with the latter tone, the *English Dialect Dictionary* supplies *mose about* ("to go about in a dull, stupid manner"). *Mosey sugar* is a confection made from the quintessentially slow *molasses*. The rather obvious source (which I've never seen printed anywhere) seems to me to be biblical, for if Moses' forty-year odyssey in the Sinai peninsula isn't a suitable metaphor for leisurely rambling, our next three thousand years aren't likely to bring a better one.

Between hay and grass is a pastoral Southwestern metaphor denoting that time of one's life between boyhood and manhood.

Y*our cotton is high* signals that

- you're thought to be either light-headed or inane.
- the whites of your eyes are unusually prominent.
- your hair is fair.
- your fly is unzipped.
- your slip's showing.

The appropriate adjective for one who's showing the whites of his eyes is *cotton-eyed*, as was the famous Joe of the square-dance tune. Inappropriate people or silly remarks are described as *cotton-headed*, but a *cottonhead* is

just a person with light-colored hair. *Your barn door's open* and *Your mule's gonna get out* are coded messages for the unclosed fly — once *It's one o'clock/two o'clock/three o'clock*, before zippers superseded buttons, then *X-Y-Z* ("*examine your zipper*") after they did. The *Dictionary of American Regional English* lists multiple sly messages for "Your slip is showing," but all are similar: *Your cotton is coming down/going down, your cotton is low/high/a-hanging/pretty/showing, your cotton's getting cheap/hanging low,* and *your cotton is below the market.* Not listed here are *It's snowin' down south* and the more elegant *Your Irish pennant is flying.*

When a Southwestern speaker stoutly upholds the veracity of what he's said by proclaiming, "If that's not so, I'll **sit up with you!**" his figure of speech is

- tutelary.
- nursemaidish.
- infernal.
- nuptial.
- funereal.

Until the beginning of the present generation the practice of *sitting up with* a corpse on the night following death was common in the American South and West. Twain's scene with Peter Wilks in *Huckleberry Finn* is a famous literary example. The deceased's friends (not family) participating in this duty would divide themselves up into watches, so that somebody was present with his body throughout the night. When as a child I questioned my father (b. 1909)

about the purpose of this custom, he told me only half jokingly that close observation was necessary to see that cats wouldn't molest the body, the heterodoxy being that the animals were strongly attracted to the recently expired person and would do him some (unnamed) harm if he were not protected.

The rite undoubtedly arose in ancient times, when man's fear of live burial was at its height, and when close observation for relatively long periods of time was necessary to determine death. My father was long dead himself by the time I had discovered this, and I'm sorry he never knew why he spent those unwelcome but dutiful vigils.

7

FROM ARKANSAS STRAWBERRIES TO FISH-FLAVORED ICE CREAM

COOKING ON THE FRONT BURNER

He knew everything about *putting the big pot in the little one* except where the expression came from.

Arkansas strawberries are

- peas.
- prostitutes.
- beans.
- birthmarks.
- acorns.

At the University of Arkansas Medical Center, where I spent my postgraduate training years, my favorite lecturer was a pediatric academician named Jim Dennis, who every now and then gave an insightful aside upon what he termed the "cult of inferiority" that has dogged the state for 150 years. He maintained that Arkansans themselves perpetuate the association of their state's name with things crude or down-at-the-heels. His view (and mine) was that children who grow up amid daily reassurances that they and their state are somehow inferior *would* be ultimately inferior. Of course he contrasted it with neighboring Texas's opposite cult, pointing out that Texans as much create for themselves a positive image — whether accurate or otherwise — as their neighbors nurture negativity.

But the unfortunate fact is historic: this lovely state is to this day linguistically enmeshed in a welter of terms for things inferior, crude, and derogatorily humorous. On rare occasions a referent with *Arkansas* is mightier than its metaphor (an *Arkansas toothpick* is a Bowie knife, and an *Arkansas dew* is a thunderstorm), but this is not usually the case. In my little East Texas town, sixty miles from the Arkansas border, the really poor part of town was called *Arkansas*. True enough, it lay on the east side of town, but that wasn't how it got its name, and everybody knew it. The *Dictionary of American Regional English* does not rec-

ord this usage (nor *Arkansas straight,* for a run of every other card in poker, 2-4-6-8-10, a worthless hand), but it does list the others.

As usual in folk phrases, food figures predominate: *Arkansas wedding cake* (cornbread), *Arkansas bananas* (papaws), *Arkansas T-bone* (salt pork), and *Arkansas strawberries* (beans). Animals are popular sources of the poor-folks metaphors, with *Arkansas lizards* (lice) and *Arkansas chicken* (sow-belly meat). A tooth-breakingly rough road of logs, a corduroy road, is alliteratively termed *Arkansas asphalt,* and an *Arkansas fire extinguisher* is a chamber pot. Nothing is sacred, not even the state's unofficial song: an *Arkansas traveler* is a minor railroad branch line, and the *Arkansas travels* is diarrhea.

The only time **horseradish** is served up with a **Mexican plate lunch** in Texas is when the two are epitomes for

- stoutness.
- leanness.
- satiation.
- heat.
- succulence.

In the rural Southwest a man described as *stout* is powerful rather than portly, and the adjective is often extended to characterize foods as well. Similes of smell that attest to strength (*Stoutern' mule's breath* and *Stout as eight acres of garbage*) mix as freely as those of taste (*Strong enough to take*

the moss off your teeth and *Stout as a Mexican plate lunch*). The authoritative, eye-watering strength of horseradish is surpassed only by a finalist's dish at the Terlingua chili cookoff: *strong enough to raise a blister on a rawhide boot.*

She *could bite through a side of bacon and not grease a gum* assures you that the woman so described is

- gossipy.
- graceless.
- greedy.
- guileless.
- gushy.

Like Whitey and his artless barbershop cronies in Ring Lardner's "Haircut," women seem no less prone than men to make fun of their own sex's physiognomies. The image of the long and solemn face of the holier-than-thou churchwoman* who *could eat oats out of a churn* is a bit more vivid but not quite as disastrous as a face like *seven miles of bad road* or the *back end of bad luck.* Her sister's teeth protruded so much that she *could eat a roastinear through a picket fence* and had a *neck as long as a well rope.* The implication in the statement about the woman with the very large mouth is that she uses it to gossip.

---

* whose nose was *stuck so high in the air that she would have drowned in a rainstorm*

He put the big pot in the little one means he

- accomplished the impossible.
- fathered children much like himself.
- distilled alcoholic spirits.
- gambled injudiciously.
- celebrated elaborately.

While all historians and folk etymologists agree upon the meaning of this phrase so commonly heard in the Southwest (i.e., to celebrate elaborately), no two agree upon the source of its original image. That the phrase is European as well (the French equivalent is *Mettre les petits plats dans les grands*), and that it's somehow from the kitchen (one southern United States addition is *dishrag and all*) are tantalizing but unhelpful details, and that the phrase is sometimes reversed (*little pot in the big one*) merely thickens the plot: gastronomes glibly supply the image of the double boiler so often used for celebratory decoctions. The reversal also fuels the fires of those who champion the whiskey distillers, who might have provided the archetypal image by decanting their product from the condenser into the tub, all in preparation for elaborate revelry.

One fanciful Texas authority has opined that *in the place of* has been elided from the original figure, and that the smaller pot on the stove was replaced by the larger one when the arrival of guests demanded the larger vessel. Knowledgeable (as well as imaginative) armchair etymologists are entreated to write the author if further theories are available; the original image remains shrouded in obscurity.

The big pot/little pot maxim simply may have been altered beyond recognition by usage. The denizens of the Southwest are famous for reshaping old saws with their own vernacular and imagery, often into aphorisms as colorful and pungent as their time-honored antecedents:

OLD	REVISED
Chinese proverb: "The journey of a thousand miles begins with the first step."	*Lick by lick, the cow ate the grindstone.*
Homer: "caught between Scylla and Charybdis"	*between a rock and a hard place*
Carroll: "grinning like a Cheshire cat"	*grinning like a jackass eating prickly pears*
Knights of the Garter: "*Honni soit qui mal y pense.*"*	*Sleep with dogs, and you'll wake up with fleas.†*
Shakespeare: "The wheel is come full circle."	*What rubs the devil's back will scratch his belly.*
Charles Kingsley: "more ways of killing a cat"	*more'n one way to break a hound from sucking eggs*
Drayton: "Since there's no help, come let us kiss and part."	*Let's us swap spit and light a shuck.*

* "Evil comes to he who evil thinks."

† really a variation from George Herbert's 1640 *Jacula Prudentum*: "He that lieth with dogs, riseth with fleas."

Aristotle: "One swallow does not make a spring."

Genesis: "In the sweat of thy face shalt thou eat bread, till thou return unto the ground."

Jonson: "Thou shouldst have looked before thou hadst leapt."

Demosthenes: "Every advantage in the past is judged in the light of the final issue."

T. Roosevelt: "Speak softly and carry a big stick."

Heracleitus: "There is nothing permanent except change."

Job: "Gird up now thy loins like a man."

Publilius Syrus: "A guilty conscience never feels secure."

Sophocles:
"A day can prostrate
  and upraise again
All that is human."

Aeschylus: "I know how men in exile feed on dreams."

It ain't spring till the bois d'arc blooms.

Root hog or die.

You can cut off a dog's tail, but you can't sew it back on.

The oprey ain't over till the fat lady sings.

Carry a window weight wrapped up in a Baptist Standard.

The sun don't shine on the same dog's ass all the time.

Get your ducks in a row.

A kicked dog'll always howl.

Chicken today, feathers tomorrow.

It was like smelling whiskey through the jailhouse door.

Aesop: "Self-conceit may lead to self-destruction."

Homer:
"Urge him with truth to frame his fair replies;
And sure he will: for Wisdom never lies."

Marvell: "till the conversion of the Jews"

Hesiod: "Oft hath even a whole city reaped the evil fruit of a bad man."

Aesop: "Beware lest you lose the substance by grasping at the shadow."

St. Matthew: "Blessed are the meek: for they shall inherit the earth."

Chaucer: "Love is blynd."

If you shovel cowshit uphill, it's liable to roll back down in your face.

The truth'll always out.

till the cows come home.

One rotten apple'll spoil a whole barrel.

Watch out you don't chase rabbits and bark at the moon.

Even a blind hog'll find an acorn once in a while.

A woman's love is like the morning dew: just as likely to fall on a horse turd as on a rose.

Les' lay on a little more kindlin' is considered an invitation to

- raise the thermostat.
- become amorous.
- tell tall tales.
- have a party.
- have another drink.

Metaphors from the hearthside have kindled colorful Southwestern speech since pioneer times. The *I'm puttin' a log on the fire* (still in use today in Oklahoma) shows the speaker's interest in what's being discussed as clearly as *Tell me more*, and *He doesn't use much kindlin' to start a fire* still describes the taciturn man. References to the kindling (or *fatwood, lighter wood*) that coaxed the initial blaze echo in *Let's yank a plank off the wall* (celebrate) in much the same way as the above sentence invites the listener to have more to drink.

Horse apples are

- dried equine droppings.
- useful in the adhesive industry.
- a little-known varmint repellent.
- the fruit of the bois d'arc tree.
- like horsefeathers: purely imaginary.

An East Texan will say *bord-ark* and a West Texan *bo-dark* as surely as the latter will say *tank* and the former *pool*.

Little known outside Texas and its surrounding states, the Osage orange (bow wood) tree acquired its folk name when early European settlers found the Indians making bows from the springy, bright yellow wood. Nineteenth-century ranchers seeded mile-long straight rows of horse apples that sprouted groves of natural dividers for their pastures, creating yet another folk name (hedge), and remnants of these giant hedges are still common in East Texas and Arkansas. The pithy, bright green apples have little other use, although many old-timers maintain that they will keep squirrels and possums out of a garage or attic. The late-spring budding habit of the bois d'arc has given rise to at least two country aphorisms: *When the bois d'arc leaf is the size of a squirrel's ear, it's time to plant* [cotton] and *It ain't spring 'til the bois d'arc blooms.*

You can hear anything in Clarksville but the jingle of change and the frying of meat means that the Texans of this town are

- reclusive.
- gossipy.
- deaf.
- poor.
- health nuts.

These words (of a speaker who is expressing doubt about a rumor he's just been told) serve a dual purpose when he suggests his needy neighbors have little else to do but gossip.

My colorful friend Jimmy Thompson, whose kin baked the bread called *the prayers of the sanctified,* spent a good many of his young years in a little town near Clarksville (Deport, Texas), and he quotes this same relative's comment about a gossipy friend: *"Well, hon, you know she never was spanked for holding her breath."* Sort of a classic country statement for one whose tongue is prone to wag.

He could sit on the fence, and the birds would feed him is an appropriate epithet for a

- closet homosexual.
- fortunate person.
- innocent flower child.
- bland half-wit.
- shiftless man.

Born in the kitchen but bearing identical meaning is the evocative *He's ridin' a gravy train with biscuit wheels.* From the outhouse comes *He could fall in an outhouse hole and come out smelling like a rose.** That the fortunate man's good luck is not altogether deserved is echoed in the anti-Newtonian description of a similarly lucky fellow: *He could fall out of a well.* My friend Logan Wilson at Greenville says, "When you're as lucky as that, cottonseed will do for brains."

---

* or *He could fall through a toilet hole and come out smelling like Evening in Paris.*

In the bayous of lower Louisiana *fish-flavored ice cream* is the ironic superlative for

- epicurism.
- intelligence.
- effrontery.
- enjoyment.
- excitement.

The Southern epicure might append *chin-lickin' good* or *larrapin'* to the best fish dish he ever *flopped a lip over*, but it wouldn't be in irony. One who's replete with *book-larnin'* might be *smart as a tree full of owls*,* but it's discretion (*A fish don't open his mouth don't get caught*) rather than intelligence that gets the piscine image. The kind of effrontery exemplified by the man who'd *fight a rattlesnake and spot him the first two bites* is summed up with only the roe (*gritty as fish eggs*), and it's the cat rather than the weird ice cream that is joyous (*happy as a tomcat in a fish market*).

Irony prevails in the superlatives for excitement: *That's about as exciting as waiting for the paint to dry/ as a mashed potato sandwich/ as watching the bumpers rust/ as fish-flavored ice cream.*

---

* sometimes *as wide awake as a tree full of owls*

Could be she's found a new dasher for her churn taken out of the kitchen becomes which of the following?

- I'm guessing she's a born-again Christian.
- Maybe she's hired a new maid.
- Might be she's in a family way.
- Perhaps she's taken a lover.
- Possibly she's found a new direction for her life.

Although the coital imagery of the milk vessel and its agitator seem readily apparent to the up-front eyes of our own generation, a grandmother of nineteenth-century Mississippi was oblivious enough of its origin to reminisce unselfconsciously upon her twice-widowed marital life with the lacteal metaphor: *"I wore out three dashers but never had but one churn."**

---

* Arkansans say, *"The post wears out before the hole"* with the same meaning.

8

FROM BULL CALVES TO TAR BRUSHES

IT'S A MATTER OF HEREDITY

Daddy was forever reminding me that *gourd vines don't grow watermelons.*

***T**hey were tarred with the same brush* gets its dark imagery from

- sheep.
- rabbits.
- thrashing.
- torture.
- mulattoes.

The very old English caveat concerning ill-advised prudences (*Don't spoil the ship for a ha'porth o' tar*) sometimes has been misinterpreted to mean something like "Don't let the ship sink for want of a few pennies worth of caulking," when in fact the *ship* is actually *sheep* — once pronounced that way in parts of England. Minor skin infections and nicks in the animals' skins are daubed with tar to promote healing, thus those *tarred with the same brush* are figuratively from the same flock, all in the same boat, or equally guilty. The fact that matted sheep's wool impregnated with tar presents a very difficult cleaning problem suggests that one who's *had the tar beat out of him* has been thoroughly thrashed. Mark Twain's punishment for the king and the duke was more severe than a thrashing, an Elizabethan form of torture appropriate for the histrionic but fraudulent pair: they were *tarred and feathered*. To have one's *head in a tar barrel* is a fate far less grim, for such a victim is merely in an embarrassing situation.

A *touch of the tar brush* is yet a different sort of daubing indeed. One human geneticist has estimated that the chances for a random white American *NOT* to have a bit of Negro blood somewhere in his lineage since Roman times is only about one in fifty, so that a little of *the mark of Cain* (so fundamentalists clamor) is far from uncommon.

We made out on middlins and son of a bitch right out of the spider can be more clearly stated:

- We drank second-rate whiskey and home brew from the still.
- We ate little but poor cuts of fried meat.
- We sold poorly refined gasoline and unprocessed crude oil.
- We traded only in moderate to low-priced stock sold over the counter.
- We smoked nothing but Bull Durham and half-cured marijuana.

These are the exact words of an elderly Oklahoma storekeeper describing his family's dirt-poor circumstances during his childhood. Warming to the subject of food, he did admit to an occasional feast: "*Come hog-killin' weather* [a sharply cool autumn day], *we'd have roastinears* [roasting ears, fresh corn on the cob] *'n lightbread* [ordinary white bread, as distinct from various cornbreads] *with some sweetnin'* [molasses]." But his family's day-to-day fare was not from the choice cuts of meat (*high on the hog*); it most often came from the middle, the sowbelly, or side meat (salt pork). Like the poor Englishmen who gave us *humble pie* (umbles, animal viscera) for humility, his family ate the pancreas, liver, sweetbreads, and other beef innards* (*son of a bitch*) stewed in the *spider*. The latter term is the name for the skillet and may have come from its association with the tripod (*spider*) that supported it over the open fire.

---

* That tripe (stomach) was often included led to the Old West expression that Stuart Flexner quoted in *Listening to America*: "A son of a bitch might not have any brains and no heart, but if he ain't got guts he ain't a son of a bitch."

In the ongoing best-phrase contest, *warming up leftover snow* comes in first as the superlative for

- poverty.
- futility.
- boredom.
- epicurism.
- nostalgia.

In addition to *pushing a wheelbarrow with rope handles,* other finalists for the epitome of futility suggested unusually bright imagery from the obscure to the really pitiful: *picking fly dookie out of black pepper, driving nails in the snow,* and *fishing with a rotten line and an empty hook.* A close contender for first place, though undeniably futile, may possess the most obscure origin in all of folk sayings: *about as fruitless as whitewashing horse manure and setting it up on end.*

Bull calves and girl babies are the curse of

- random genetics.
- the stockman and the nameless.
- the lowborn and the untitled.
- the well-to-do and mercantile.
- the poor and agrarian.

Many adages of the Southwest echo the oft-misquoted Beatitude suggesting the poor will fare better in other worlds (*A plow hand is taller on his knees than a rich man on*

his feet), although the admission is often a rueful one (*There's nothing shameful about being poor, but sometimes it's damned inconvenient*). A man *as poor as Job's turkey* has neither *a pot to pee in nor a window to throw it out of;* in fact *he's too poor even to pay attention.* But the beleaguered and impoverished preserve their self-esteem (*too poor to paint and too proud to whitewash*), their complaisance (*Poor folks have poor ways*), and their sense of humor (*The rich get richer and the poor get children*).

He didn't suck it all out of his thumb is another Southwestern version of

- As the twig is bent, so grows the vine.
- Environment is more important than heredity.
- He didn't come by it naturally.
- Fruit won't fall far from the tree.

Only the thought and the end-line rhyme are preserved in the commonly misquoted couplet from *Moral Essays*:
　'Tis education forms the common mind:
　Just as the twig is bent the tree's inclined.
Pope gives more credit to one's environment than to his genes. The thumb-sucking expression supports the conviction behind another common figure for genetically acquired traits learned *at the mother's breast* (i.e., "come by naturally") and thus has once again reframed the ubiquitous *Blood is thicker than water* with *Fruit won't fall far from the tree.*

A *box of rocks* and *a barrel of hair* have tied as superlatives for

- worthlessness.
- superfluity.
- silence.
- innocence.
- stupidity.

Unsorted submissions to an unscholarly but lively fill-in-the-blank contest ran thus:

He was so dumb that he didn't know _____

- *any more than to do what you told him.*
- *beans.*
- *beef from bees' wool.*
- *'c'mere' from 'sic'im'.*
- *chicken doo from chicken salad.*
- *crap from wild honey.*
- *diddley squat.*
- *enough to come in out of the rain.*
- *east from west / north from south.*
- *fettucini Alfredo from stuffing.*
- *the first thing about fishing / writing / etc.*
- *good from bad.*
- *his left from his right.*
- *his ass from a hole in the ground.*
- *his ass from a rattlesnake hole.*
- *his ass from first base.*
- *his ass from Grand Canyon.*

- *nothin' from nothin'.*
- *pea turkey doo.*
- *pine trees from pineapples.*
- *shit from Shinola.*
- *split-pea soup from honey.*
- *the time of day.*
- *that any more than the man in the moon.*
- *up from down.*
- *what day/week/month/year it is.*
- *which way's up.*

In addition to *dumb as a box of rocks, as a barrel of hair, as a dog about Sunday, as a goose in a new world,* and *as a flock of guineas,* variations included *He's so dumb they had to burn down the high school to get him out, If all my brains was ink, I couldn't dot an* i, *If all my brains was dynamite, I couldn't blow my nose,* and *He was so dumb he couldn't pour piss out of a boot with a hole in the toe and directions on the heel.*

T he Great White Whale and a dog named Hector both figure in superlatives for

- ferocity.
- vindictiveness.
- torment.
- imagination.
- antiquity.

In casting about for descriptions of things remote, speakers have invoked (as usual) the world of animals (*since*

Hector was a pup, since Moby Dick was a minnow, and *for a coon's age*), the calendar (*until the second Tuesday of next week, for a month of Sundays,* and *until the first cold day in July*), and the netherworld (*till hell freezes over, since the devil was a little boy,* and *till hell's no hotter'n a candle*). A man may grow *so old he doesn't buy green bananas any more, so old he won't read a continued piece in a magazine,* or even *so old he looks like one clean shirt would do him*. The only phrase that tops *nine years older than baseball* is the ultimate superlative for antiquity: *older'n dirt*.

The appellation of **son of a gun,** the practice of **snuffing** somebody, and the phrase **born to the purple** all draw their original imagery from

- the labor room.
- the underworld.
- Billy the Kid.
- the barroom.
- the Vatican.

Admiral W.H. Smyth's nineteenth-century *Sailor's Word Book* defines a *son of a gun* simply as anybody born at sea. Perhaps it is merely embroidery upon his story that the mother of such a lad had had her labor enhanced by firing a naval cannon over her accouchement bed to hasten the baby's delivery. Whether the whole story or any part of it is apocryphal, this is the recorded source of *son of a gun,* a phrase now used in the Southwest most often as an exclamation, commonly as a term of endearment, only occasionally as a euphemism, and never in its original sense.

On land, an obstetrical delivery in frontier times was sometimes hastened by *snuffing,* in which judicious pinches of that product were given to the confined patient to induce sneezing, which in turn was thought to speed up labor. The therapeutic efficacy was probably about on the order of that of the *hair of the dog.*

Born to the purple descends from the Byzantine *born in the porphyry,* the purple feldspar stone with which the royal labor room was decorated. Such a fortunate latter-day infant is born to parents of wealth rather than nobility.

Match the words and phrases on the left with their meanings on the right by writing the appropriate letters in the blanks. Look for the acrostic.

___ *bathroom stationery*   A. a sack or bag
___ *poke*   B. moonshine whiskey
___ *coon-ass*   C. a Cajun
___ *mountain oysters*   D. fried possum
___ *mountain dew*   E. *a cracker*
___ Georgia native   F. a coyote
___ *Alabama wool*   G. a sandstorm
___ *black-eyed Susan*   H. a prostitute
___ *Arizona tenor*   I. a revolver
___ *white lightnin'*   J. toilet paper
___ *Arkansas racehorse*   K. sheep or hog testes
___ poor white man   L. a razorback hog
                                           M. a tubercular
                                           N. cotton underwear

If you saw the acrostic, write the next line: _____*

Jack be quick.

9

FROM
ALL WOOL AND A YARD WIDE
TO
THE HIGH FIVE

IT'S A MATTER OF CHARACTER

Daddy warned me: *"Don't ever get in a pissin' contest with a skunk."*

 two-button man describes one who's

- stylishly and expensively dressed.
- well-to-do and influential.
- of little consequence.
- conservative and cautious.
- remarkably closemouthed and discreet.

That the buttons of this virile metaphor are situated upon the trousers (in lieu of a zipper) rather than the shirt or coat gives the reader a rough idea of its vintage, for one's fly is seldom secured with buttons nowadays. A man who can accomplish his errand at the chic sales by undoing only two buttons cannot be of much consequence, a real lightweight in fact. A *four-button man* is quite a different fellow indeed.

ny resident east of the Mississippi who is **GTT** is presumed to be

- among the nouveaux riches.
- a Southerner at heart.
- wicked.
- deceased.
- part black.

Authors from Twain to Faulkner have used *GTT* for their characters' whereabouts. Whether the fleeing one has repaired to the next county on horseback or to South America on a New Orleans freighter, his *Gone to Texas*

label marks his motives as dishonorable, although they may have ranged from an unhappy love affair to a suspicion of murder. A little like many earlier Europeans who sought refuge in the New World, such a man had to have *something* about him at least a little suspect, since he had chosen flight to such a raffish place.

The renegade would often choose for his new life a *summer name,* a pseudonym or alias whereby he could avoid recognition in his adopted home.

ny woman who is ***stiff in the heels*** is

- putting on airs.
- a poor dancer.
- impoverished.
- well-to-do.
- immoral.

Well-heeled nowadays invariably means moneyed, but the phrase began its career with an entirely different denotation. In the nineteenth century a man described as *heeled* was one who bore arms. A *well-heeled* gunman wore a revolver on each hip, not on each heel. The figure came from the ancient gamecock pit, where the feet of fighting chickens were fitted with metal spurs with which to rip their opponents. In our "more sophisticated" century, perhaps one's most effective armament is cash, so that the phrase now refers only to this sort of equipage. It's the *round-heeled woman* who's immoral and the poor one who's *down at the heels.*

Hickey is

- a space between the teeth left by a missing tooth.
- the penalty in a game when a player fails to make his bid.
- a skin tag, pimple, or zit.
- a tool with which to bend pipe.
- any unspecified object, a "whatchamacallit."
- a domino game.
- a "love bite" acquired during sexual play.
- an electrical fitting.
- an adjective for a rube or country bumpkin.
- a speck on an engraving that remains after the etch.
- tipsy but not quite drunk.

It seems ironic, given the omnivorousness and scope of the 600,000-word English language, that a single word should possess eleven distinct meanings — and even more ironic that the heritage of so many of them has been in the West, where rough-and-ready wordsmiths have seldom been loathe to make up a new word to fit the novel object or situation.

What common, two-syllabled English word may be defined in these (as well as at least twenty other) terms?

- a detonator in the form of a metal dart, used to set off dynamite in an oil well
- an iron grate for an outdoor fire
- a railroad handcar
- a logging sled

- a highly seasoned turkey or chicken leg
- a platform on a cable over a stream
- a large machine equipped with knives or spikes for ripping up rags
- a jointed tool with which to unstop a clogged drain
- a device to destroy fishnets
- a pressman's assistant*

Of these five similar similes, two have identical meanings. Pick the pair.

- *tight as the paper on the wall*
- *tight as Dick's hatband*
- *tight as Romeo and Juliet*
- *tight as a mink*
- *tight as O'Reilly's balls*

My Texas-born grandmother's simile to describe the fit of my often outgrown clothes was lost on my childhood ears, for until I was an adult I thought that her *Dick's hatband* was some sort of musical organization. Much remote from her use of the adjective (as snug-fitting) is *tight as a mink* (or *lord*), meaning tipsy, as is *tight as Romeo and Juliet* (sympathetic). Of course the first and the last phrases describe the really hard-core, Scrooge-like parsimony of the man whose wallet emits moths when he opens it.

---

* This and each of the other nine definitions is, for various though not always fathomable reasons, a *devil*.

She's all wool and a yard wide means she's

- sanctimonious and narrow-minded.
- well-to-do and generous.
- disorganized and deluded.
- upper-class and intolerant.
- genuine and undesigning.

From the hides of sheep, folk sayings have shorn a mixed bag: figures denoting deception (*pull the wool over one's eyes*), impracticality (*wooly headed*), and witlessness (*wool gathering; fleecy reasoning*) are as numerous as those suggesting authenticity (*all wool, a yard long and a yard wide*), substance (*great cry and little wool*),* and thoroughness (*dyed in the wool*). The last phrase describes the colorfast property of cloth made from pre-dyed wool as distinct from the piece-dyed variety, so that a *dyed-in-the-wool Democrat* is at least as rock-ribbed as a *yellow-dog Democrat* (who'd presumably vote for such an animal if its name appeared on that party's ticket) or a *dog-collar Democrat*.

From the processing (perhaps with a *devil*) of this material comes the rough-and-tumble image of the rueful man who places second in a fistfight: "He *wooled* me around like a dog with a bone."† And beneath the finished product shambles the *wool-hat boy* who's no less the yokel than his off-season analogue, the rube who *wore his straw hat to a Christmas tree*.

---

* identical to *all talk and no action*

† This man came out worse than the fellow in the shorter fight: *"He whipped me before he got mad."*

He came close to the dollar knife describes a man who's

- just been shaved by a skillful barber.
- been sexually indiscreet.
- fallen upon hard times.
- just missed his objective.
- been injured by a cut-rate surgeon.

The poker player who's just missed a straight flush by one card, a suitor who's been turned down by a beauty queen who really thought over his proposal, and the coach whose team made it to state finals only to lose the game — each of these unfortunates has just barely missed his objective, that is, has *come close to the dollar knife.* The figure of speech arose from the coin-operated game of yesteryear's carnivals, in which the player manipulated a mechanical claw over a glass-enclosed bin of prizes. Nestled amid the heap of gum balls and plastic toys was the then-expensive *dollar knife,* an elusive treasure that has become the metaphor for the near miss.

The original *boogeyman,* with whom a Southwestern mother frightens her children, hailed from

- Bulgaria, via *Bulgarian.*
- France, via *bourgeoisie.*
- Cajun Louisiana, via *boogaloo.*
- England, via *bugger.*

European mothers' admonitions to their children have lingered in skeletal forms, ostensibly because of exclu-

sively oral importation, after their trackless but fascinating journeys. The French mother's ancient and ominous *Tel rit au matin qui pleure au soir** is echoed only in form by the common phrase of the East Texas mother who warns her pyromaniacal child, "If you play with fire before sundown, you'll wet the bed before dawn."

It was the French mother of several generations past who first borrowed her image from the Bulgarian mercenary soldiers whose black beards and fierce faces must indeed have presented a frightening sight. "You'd better be good," she admonished, "or the *bulgare* will get you." Her *byool-gher* has traveled down many a linguistic byroad to reach the *boogieman, boogeyman,* or *booger* of today.

juke joint gets its name from

- a fictitious surname implying lower-class origins.
- an African word for whorehouse.
- the mechanical record player once seen there.
- a type of neck wound inflicted with a knife.
- the inferior marijuana with which it's made.

In an 1877 treatise, R.L. Dugdale made up the name *Juke* for families of criminal and impoverished sociopaths he believed changed but little with successive generations.

---

* *Laugh before breakfast, and you'll cry before dark.*

But his cognomen stemmed from a word much older: the *juke house* (brothel) of North Carolina's Gullahs was imported with eighteenth-century African slaves. That the coin-operated phonograph early found its way to such unsavory resorts is suggested by its name, and one who's been stabbed in the neck has been *juged* (from *jugular*), not *juked*, the latter a verb for one who drank and cavorted in sleazy taverns.

One who *has calluses on his feet* is

- ungodly.
- unvirtuous.
- unschooled.
- unmanly.
- untimely.

One who *shows his cloven foot* discloses his illicit plans in the ungodly manner of the cloven-hooved one, only a little worse than the *round-heeled* woman of easy virtue, whose promiscuous behavior of lying down at the slightest inducement has shaped her *rocker-bottom feet*.

In keeping with their disdain for all things sinistral, the Romans deemed it unlucky to enter a room or a house with the left foot first, and their reluctance was passed on to later courtiers who always *put their best foot forward*. Only the unschooled would risk his *good footing* with such a gaucherie. One who makes such a foolish error might just as well follow the unmanly course of *showing a clean pair of heels* (run away, escape).

105

Citing a citizen of the Ozarks of 1910, Frederic Cassidy explains in his *Dictionary of American Regional English* that having *calluses on one's feet* denotes a baby born to a mother married less than nine months. Sometimes *born with burnt feet,* such an infant has presumably damaged his feet making the usual nine-month trip in a shorter period of time.

The phrase *lopes and smokes* describes

- antelopes and cougars.
- Mexicans and blacks.
- space.
- time.
- distance.

In a 1970 article in the *Silver City Press,* New Mexico cowboy and feature writer Allton Turner explained how the Appalachian measure of distance — so many *whoops and hollers* — has traveled west to become *lopes and smokes.* Gal*loping* one's horse precluded smoking, an activity pursued when the cowboy rested his winded animal by allowing it to walk. Such intervals became a measure of distance. Mr. Turner's article didn't say how far one *lope and smoke* is, and I can't guess intelligently.

Turner was the only writer I ever read who was able to explain convincingly the exact origin of *sucking on the hind teat.* Although this expression is occasionally used in the sense of *cooking on the front burner* (i.e., in a favorable position), it most often implies a disadvantageous site. The

New Mexico man described with authority how a motherless calf sought to steal milk from a cow walking with her own calf at her side. Because this had to be accomplished with the culprit's head between the cow's hind legs, he didn't get much. One who *sucks the hind teat* is in a perilous and profitless predicament.

The Robinsons got well in the drugstore business means that the family

- made its fortune (honestly) in pharmaceuticals.
- manufactured (profitably) illicit drugs.
- recouped their (sideline) losses by filling prescriptions.
- made money (unaccountably) composing western songs.
- recovered (from the Depression) illegitimately.

My friend Jimmy Thompson's eccentric and unsystematic linguistic investigations in East Texas uncovered a curious association: The same areas that use *soon* in the sense of *early* ("I have to drive to Dallas *soon* in the morning" or "Aunt Jessie called us *soon* this morning to tell us little Owen was sick") are those in which *got well* is most often substituted for *made money*.* It's as if those who are impecunious are somehow most often prone to ill health.

---

* perhaps a pile of it *a show dog couldn't jump over*

At least in the Southwest, a **New York minute** is the epitome of

- small size.
- procrastination.
- speed.
- sluggishness.
- ease.

The blinding speed of the *New York minute* must have grown out of the rapid rate of Easterners' speech rather than their sense of time, because I've invariably found that a New Yorker's (or a Londoner's, for that matter) "ten-minute walk" (as an estimation of distance) is closer to *a lope and smoke* than it is to *a whoop and a holler*. A *New York minute* passes *fast as greased lightnin'*, *quick as a duck on a June bug*, *faster 'n a scalded cat*, and even *'fore God can get the news*.

He's in the high five describes a man

- who earns more than $50,000 a year.
- who's been arrested on serious charges.
- who belongs to the exclusive upper class.
- who's making use of a public rest room.
- deceased and buried in a prestigious cemetery.

In his *From Blinky to Blue-John*: A Word Atlas of Northeast Texas,* linguist Fred Tarpley shows that though the *high five* as a euphemism for *jail* stemmed from a courthouse like the one in Paris, Texas, with its detention facility on the fifth floor, the term (occasionally just *high fi*) is used throughout the northeast corner of the state, even by those citizens of counties whose jails are separate buildings or located on other floors.

---

* *Blinky* describes milk in the early stages of souring; *blue-john* is milk with the cream removed.

10

FROM A BARREL OF SNAKES TO SCARCE-HIPPED HOGS

BEASTS DOMESTIC AND OTHERWISE

Daddy's favorite expression for unreadiness was *The hog is dead and the water's not hot.*

A *latch on the outhouse door* is the epitome of

- discretion.
- knowledge (of gossip).
- convenience.
- superfluity.
- reliability.

Linguistically distinctive for its convenience (*handy as a latch on the outhouse door*), this device is just ahead of *handy as pockets on a shirt* and *handy as one-syllable words*, and it's just behind *handy as sliced bread* and *handy as a rope at a lynchin'*. Ironic similes are just as popular: *about as handy as hip pockets on a shroud, about as handy as a turd in a punch bowl*, and *about as handy as hip pockets on a hog*.

A *chunk floater,* a *fence lifter,* and a *frog strangler* are three

- items of fishing tackle.
- varieties of kite bridles.
- tools for working with barbed wire.
- country words for cravats, men's ties.
- various terms describing weather.

Much of the Southwest lies in an area of sparse rainfall where drought is common. Perhaps its climatic circumstances combined with its citizens' penchant for the the-

atrical superlative to produce the many figures for the torrential rainstorm, however uncommon it may be.* It's no less puzzling why beasts are so often inundated (*toad strangler, duck drowner, goose choker*) than how such unusual items are figuratively said to fall (It's rainin' *bullfrogs and heifer yearlings/horse apples and pigs' knuckles/pitchforks and Negro babies*). The cloudburst that grows into a *stump mover, sod soaker, log roller, gully washer,* or *dam buster* reaches its ultimate force (at least for imagery) when it's likened to *a cow peein' on a flat rock*.

A *barrel of snakes* wins first prize in a superlative contest to establish the epitome of

- slipperiness.
- slickness.
- danger.
- deviousness.
- sliminess.

It's the snake's ever-so-distant cousin that gets the nod for the highest degree of slipperiness (the same figure of speech placed second for obscenity as well), *slippery as an eel in a barrel of snot,* with the similar *slick as a booger on a doorknob* earning a first for both slickness *and* obscenity. *Slicker'n a slop jar* was only a distant second, probably

---

* "You know that last year Lubbock had an annual rainfall of twelve inches?"
 "Uh-huh, I was out there that day."

because this appurtenance is no longer under every bed in America.

Favorite Central Texas superlatives for "crooked" — playing upon the ambiguity of that adjective (i.e., devious) reflect its geography and flora: *crooked as the Brazos River* and *crooked as a live oak limb* were well behind the time-honored *dog's hind leg* but ahead of *crooked as a box of fishhooks*. Unplaced in the contest but my favorite for imagery was the evocative *crooked as the shade of a posthole auger*.

In East Texas **hoss-high and bull-strong** typically describes

- bourbon with a really authoritative taste.
- the quintessential Marlboro man.
- a curvaceous woman.
- a healthy cow dog.
- an outdoor building.

Perhaps in linguistic reparation for having likened the figure of a seductive woman to an inanimate structure (*She's built like a brick outhouse*), folk vernacular has this time used the mammalian metaphor for a man-made structure, since any stoutly constructed outdoor edifice,* from a trestle bridge to a pole barn, can receive this country encomium.

---

* although the corral was very likely the first structure so described

A *cockroach in a hot skillet* is the epitome of

- futility.
- hopelessness.
- uselessness.
- evanescance.
- restlessness.

Just why the animal world is so often invoked for epitomes is unclear; maybe the eye of man is more candid when he sees himself reflected in the human remnants of the "lower" animals. The abject futility of *a bug arguing with a chicken* makes a much brighter image than simply *whistling Dixie,* although they imply the same thing, and it's too painful to imagine any human condition more hopeless than *a grasshopper in a henhouse.* The heights, or depths, of uselessness are simply grotesque in a *flat-chested stripper.* However, they take on a bit more color with the shift to an animal simile: *Useless as the teats on a boar hog* or *useless as a marriage license for a tomcat* express no less unserviceability than do *useless as taking a chicken to church* or *useless as taking a dog to Sunday school.* Even the epitome for evanescence (*He won't last till the water gets hot*) was born in the hog-slaughtering yard. The grossness of understatement of *restless as a cockroach in a hot skillet* is matched only by the brightness of its animal-world imagery.

A *bat's ear* is a Southwestern superlative for

- leanness.
- keenness.
- meanness.
- cleanness.

Albeit to my knowledge yet unplayed, a game in which contestants fill in the blank after "He was as thin as ____" might glean as many entries as the "Dumb as a ____" survey already conducted. *He was so thin he had to walk by twice to make a shadow* has been used to describe both a man and his *scarce-hipped* hogs. Perhaps because one's slenderness is most apparent when he's at his ablutions, such similes are often set there: *He was so thin he had to dodge around in the shower to get wet, He was so thin he always got out of the tub before he pulled the plug,* and *He was so thin he could take a shower in a gun barrel* are examples of this genre. Sometimes the imagery is simple (*He was so thin you had to shake the sheets to find him*) and sometimes complex (*He was so thin you could mark lines on him and use him for a yardstick**).

It's the *eagle's eye* that's known for keenness and the *gnat's whisker* for little room to spare, and anything from a reputable business to a burned-off pasture can be described *as clean as a dog's tooth*. Reserved for a superlative for leanness is the diaphanous ear of nature's distinctive flying mammal: *thin as a bat's ear*.

---

* or *so thin that if he turned sideways and stuck out his tongue, you could use him for a zipper*

A *restless mule in a tin barn* is the epitome of

- stubbornness.
- vindictiveness.
- dishonor.
- narcissism.
- cacophony.

Storied for his recalcitrant nature, the mule has been featured in *stubborn as a blue-nosed mule/government mule/army mule,* and no less an author than William Faulkner has written of his vindictiveness, saying one would work tractably for a generation in exchange for just one chance to kick his owner in the head. One who *shoes his own mule* misappropriates funds of which he is the trustee, an unquestionably dishonorable deed. The imagery of *loping one's mule* (masturbating) titillates even the feeblest imagination.

Only the cacophony remains, and *noisy as a restless mule in a tin barn* makes the simile with redoubtable imagery, although perhaps not with as much as *noisy as two skeletons fornicating on a tin roof* in the same vein, a noise *so loud one can't hear himself think.*

Metaphysical expressions like the last phrase seem perennially popular in Southwestern folk sayings, like the poor farmer whose *tires were so thin you could see the air in them.* Supernatural figures run from meteorologic (*It's so dry the trees are following the dogs around for water*) and anatomic (She cooks real *stick-to-your-ribs* food and *His eyes were bigger than his stomach*) to mathematical (*These eggs are so big it won't take many to make a dozen*) and astronomical (*They lived so far out in the woods that the sun set between their*

117

house and town). Those who coin such improbabilities are so logically inept they *couldn't knock a hole in the wind with a sackful of hammers.*

In central Arkansas the word ***peckerwood*** is

- a curious inversion of *woodpecker,* a bird.
- an adjective meaning itinerant, fly-by-night.
- a Black English pejorative for a white man, a "honkie."
- an unsuccessful and impoverished farmer, a sharecropper.

A small and temporary sawmill, usually set up in a central location to take advantage of the easily accessible timber around it, typically turns out railroad ties and wood pulp for a few months and then moves on to the deeper woods. Such a shoestring enterprise is called a *peckerwood mill*, differentiating it from the larger and more permanent wood-processing plant. It may have acquired its humble name from the archetypal, out-of-luck farmer who first turned his hand to this alternate occupation. Although such a man would never call himself a *peckerwood,* he might very well apply it (though for no discernible reason) to a sort of bird that attacked his trees.

Maybe the linguistic inversion of the word elements (by a black speaker, as a word for a white man) is simply a dialectal and racial rebuttal for *blackbird* (a Negro) — wearing a disguise in the manner of *ofay,* an exact synonym for *peckerwood* and a pejorative for a white person clad but thinly in pig Latin.

t's time to talk turkey came into Southwestern vernacular from

- the pilgrims.
- an American Indian.
- Istanbul, Turkey.
- David Crockett.
- a theatrical critic.

Mitford Mathews' *Dictionary of Americanisms* quotes an 1830 *N.Y. Mirror* story recounting the division of game between a white hunter and his Indian companion. The former said, "You may have your choice, you take the crow and I'll take the turkey, or if you'd rather, I'll take the turkey and you take the crow."* It was Wampum's answer that coined the phrase: "Ugh! you no talk turkey to me a bit."

The feckless turkey of folk phrase is not unlike the ox. Born a misnomer (a native North American, probably from Mexico and certainly not Turkey†), the bird has found himself in phrases connoting everything from benevolent drunkenness (*to have a turkey on one's back*) to abject poverty (*poor as Job's turkey*), the latter term from Thomas Haliburton's Sam Slick, who said the impoverished bird had but one tail feather and had to lean on the fence just to gobble.

---

* An early recipe for cooking crow recommends boiling the bird thirty-six hours and then adding a fist-sized rock and continuing. When you can stick a fork in the rock, the crow's done.

† first imported to England from Africa, by way of Turkey, hence the name

Identified in the nineteenth century with advantage and reward (and occasionally still heard in this sense: *you get the turkey* [prize]), the turkey had by the 1940s become synonymous with a theatrical or motion-picture failure.* Nowadays the foolish, uninitiated, or unfashionable person has become a *turkey,* only a linguistic half step above the *nerd.*

A *pregnant fox in a forest fire* has found a place in the lingo of the Southwest as the epitome of

- heat.
- speed.
- hopelessness.
- nervousness.
- misfortune.

Much of the language's color and many of its brightest imageries (along with not a few of its obscenities) have been happily shoehorned into its similes. Something can be *as hot as*

- *a two-dollar pistol.*
- *a pot of collard greens / stewed apples / corn dumplings.*
- *hell on Sunday.*
- *a two-dollar whore on the fourth of July.*
- *a depot stove.*
- *the hinges of hell.*

---

* or a stale joke (*old turkey*), a "chestnut"

- *a pair of jumper cables at a Negro funeral.*
- *a billy goat in a pepper patch.*
- *a fresh-fornicated fox in a forest fire.*

Someone can be *as nervous as a*

- *whore in church.**
- *peach orchard sow.*
- *dog passing peach seeds.*
- *bastard at a family reunion.*
- *pregnant donkey in a traffic jam.*
- *man with a pacemaker at a microwave cookoff.*
- *long-tailed cat in a room full of rocking chairs.*
- *pregnant fox in a forest fire.*

My **biddies was right thrifty but down in their gitalongs** is a woman's comment about her

- economical but jobless sons.
- trim but spiritless friends.
- scrimping but indolent daughters.
- slim but slow ponies.
- fat but crippled chickens.

Biddies as a folk name for hens or other fowl may have come about from their feeder's call to them, "Hey bid-

---

* who might be *so nervous she could thread a sewing machine with it running*

dybiddybiddy!" Although the call is in turn likely to be onomatopoeic.*

The British *biddy* is not a hen but an Irish maidservant (from *Bridget*), but American usage for a person is invariably preceded by *old* and applied only to a gossipy old woman.

That *thrift* (Old Norse *thrīask,* to thrive) meant flourishing before it came to mean economy should not be surprising. Just as *stout* implied power before it euphemized obesity, the folk use seems to have clung to the older denotation.

Another noteworthy example of this persistence is the use of the word *snuff* in folk phrases. The eighteenth- and early nineteenth-century habit of "dipping" or inhaling pulverized tobacco was not only socially acceptable but fashionable, so that the figures of speech employing the word were uniformly positive. The *Dictionary of Americanisms* quotes early 1800s speakers' *in great snuff* and *in high snuff* as figures of elaborate dress and high fashion, and to this day *up to snuff* means straightforward and honest. The ensuing two centuries have found the habit disagreeable and unhealthy, but the wholesomeness of its phrases lingers on unaltered.

Although a few Southwestern speakers acknowledge that *down in one's gitalongs* can be extended to include a reference to low-back pain, most feel that the word's use is restricted, whether describing humans or chickens, to trouble with the legs.

---

* In fact some philologists maintain that almost every word in every language began as either an onomatopoeia or a metaphor.

Gone where the woodbine twines and the whangdoodle mourneth for its mate

- signals the withdrawal of a player from a hand of poker.
- describes the whereabouts of a misplaced article or missing person.
- was Jim Fisk's 1870 explanation of missing gold market money.
- describes something that nowadays would be "down the tubes."

All poker players (all the good ones, at least) have to say "I drop out" so often that they seek variations with the same meaning. I first heard this alternate from a very old cardplayer who grew up in Colorado and had a fine memory and ear for the phrases of the nineteenth-century West, where so many such grandiloquent replacements were born. The flavor of the frontier is unmistakable, the mixing of the Shakespearean pastoral image of the woodbine (honeysuckle) with the whangdoodle (gizmo, doohickey) of the American Southwest.

In his *Heavens to Betsy!*, Charles Earle Funk remembers the phrase, with a slight variation (... *mourneth for his firstborn*), from his boyhood Ohio of the 1880s, writing that he and his brother used it to describe the whereabouts of any unaccountably missing object or person. Along with many other phraseologists, Funk quotes the infamous Jim Fisk, who was asked by a congressional committee to account for fifty million dollars of gold market money, missing after the 1869 crash. *"It's gone where the woodbine twineth,"* Fisk answered. When a committee member requested clarification of his metaphor, Fisk interpreted, *"Up the spout."*

It's time to put the bricks in the floor demands

- return to serious matters.
- immediate departure.
- on-the-spot repairs.
- prompt resumption of work.
- forthright honesty.

The former citizen of New Mexico who in 1988 used this phrase to describe her husband's hasty departure might have been startled to know the antiquity of her figure, for it was more than a few hundred years ago that servants of the gentry first heated bricks in preparation for a journey. These flannel-wrapped footwarmers were deposited on the floor of milady's carriage or sleigh, and since they didn't stay warm very long, their placement signaled the time for prompt departure. Heated bricks, cold carriages, and unpleasant travel are long gone; only the useful and reminiscent phrase remains.

It's time to put the bricks in the floor.

INVITATION

If you have a favorite phrase or word from American folk vernacular that you would be willing to contribute to further editions of this book, you are invited to write or call the author at 10 N.E. First Street, Paris, Texas 75460, telephone (214) 784-4992.

If you answered every question in the book correctly on the first reading, write or call for a phrase guaranteed to stump *anybody*.

 BIBLIOGRAPHY

Atwood, E. Bagby. *The Regional Vocabulary of Texas.* Austin: University of Texas Press, 1962.

Benthul, Herman F. *Wording Your Way Through Texas.* Burnet, Texas: Eakins Press, 1981.

Black, Donald C. *Spoonerisms, Sycophants, and Sops.* New York: Harper & Row, 1988.

Bowman, Bob. *I Ain't Sure I Understand Everything I Know About This.* Lufkin, TX.: Best of East Texas Pub., 1985.

Bowman, Bob. *If I Tell You a Hen Dips Snuff....* Lufkin, TX.: Lufkin Printing Company, 1981.

Brewer, Ebenezer C. *Brewer's Dictionary of Phrase and Fable.* New York: Harper & Row, 1979.

Cassidy, Frederic G., ed. *Dictionary of American Regional English.* Cambridge: Harvard University Press, Belknap Press, 1985.

Dickson, Paul. *Words.* New York: Delacorte, 1982.

Farmer, J.S., and W.E. Henley. *A Dictionary of Slang.* Ware, Hertfordshire, England: Wordsworth Editions, 1987.

Flexner, Stuart B. *Listening to America.* New York: Simon & Schuster, 1982.

Funk, Charles E. *Heavens to Betsy!* New York: Perennial Library, 1986.

Funk, Charles E. *A Hog on Ice.* New York: Harper Colophon Books, 1985.

Funk, Charles E. *Horsefeathers & Other Curious Words.* New York: Perennial Library, 1986.

Funk, Charles E. *Thereby Hangs a Tale.* New York: Perennial Library, 1985.

Funk, Wilfred. *Word Origins and Their Romantic Stories.* New York: Grosset & Dunlap, 1950.

Grose, Francis. *1811 Dictionary of the Vulgar Tongue.* London: Bibliophile Books, 1984.

Holt, Alfred. *Phrase and Word Origins.* New York: Dover, 1961.

Ladwig, Tom. *How To Talk Dirty Like Grandad.* Little Rock: Rose Publishing Company, 1985.

Leach, Maria, ed. *Funk & Wagnalls Standard Dictionary of Folklore, Mythology, and Legend.* New York: Funk & Wagnalls, 1949.

Mathews, Mitford M., ed. *A Dictionary of Americanisms.* Chicago: University of Chicago Press, 1951.

Mencken, H.L. *The American Language.* New York: Knopf, 1977.

Morris, William, and Mary Morris. *Dictionary of Word and Phrase Origins.* New York: Harper & Row, 1962.

Partridge, Eric. *Origins.* New York: Macmillan, 1966.

Sale, Charles (Chic). *The Specialist.* St. Louis: Specialist Publishing Company, 1929.

Spears, Richard A. *Slang and Euphemism.* New York: New American Library, 1981.

Syatt, Dick. *Like We Say Back Home.* Secaucus, N.J.: Citadel Press, 1987.

Tallman, Marjorie. *Dictionary of American Folklore.* New York: Philosophical Library, 1959.

Tarpley, Fred. *From Blinky to Blue-John.* Wolfe City, TX: The University Press, 1970.

Whiting, Bartlett J. *Early American Proverbs and Proverbial Phrases.* Cambridge: Harvard University Press, Belknap Press, 1977.

Wilder, Roy, Jr. *You All Spoken Here.* New York: Penguin, 1984.

INDEX

Abbett, Spencer, vii
Acorn, 43, 80
Adam's off-ox, 5, 34
Aeschylus, 79
Aesop, 80
Aggies, 65-66
Alabama wool, 96
All got up, 54
All wool and a yard wide, 102
Allopathy, 44
Ameche, 47
Animal calls, 17
Apple, rotten, 80
Aristotle, 79
Arizona tenor, 96
Arkansas . . ., vii, 74-75, 96
Armadillo, 34, 35
Asafetida, 50
Ass from . . ., 92
Ass-kickin' contest, 29
Atwood, E. Bagby, 18, 17
Aunt Maudie, O lawdy, 34

Baby fingers!, 23
Back row, sits on the, 64
Bacon, 76
Bahmanishous, 25
Baking a cake, 68
Balderdash, 52
Ball the jack in his rod, 27-28
Balls, 45, 101
Baloney, Floyd Ables', 57
Bananas, green, 94
Baptist, 41, 65-66
Baptist Standard, 79
Barbed wire, 59
Bark at the moon, 38, 80
Barking up the wrong tree, 6
Barn door's open, 71
Barrel(s), 15, 88, 92, 113-114
Baseball, nine years older than, 94
Bass, sings, 64
Bastard, 55, 121
Bathroom stationery, 96
Bat's ear, 116
Beat with . . ., 18, 42
Beau-catchers, 47
Beef from bees' wool, 92

Beer, vii, 52
Before God can get the news, 108
Belly, 8, 89
Ben's . . ., 34, 35
Besom, jump the, 51
Bessie bug, crazy as a , 34
Between a rock and a hard place, 78
Between hay and grass, 69-70
Bicycle, fish needs a, 32
Biddies, 121-122
Billets-doux, 47
Billy Blue Hill, 15
Birds would feed him, 83
Biscuit wheels, 83
Blackbird, 118
Black-eyed Susan, 96
Blanket, wrong side of, 56
Blazes, drunk as, 33
Blind hog, 43
Blister on a rawhide boot, raise a, 76
Blood is thicker than water, 91
Blossom, Texas, vii
Blow my nose, 93
Blue-gummer, 24-25
Boar, 30, 32
Bois d'arc, 79, 81-82
Booger on a doorknob, 113
Boogeyman, 103-104
Boot with a hole in the toe, 93
Born . . ., 94-95, 106
Bowman, Bob, 15
Box of . . ., 92, 114
Brains was . . ., 93
Bread, 67
Brick(s), 16, 114, 124
Broke as . . ., 29, 56
Broke her knee/leg/ankle, 68
Broom, jumped the, 51
Brush, tarred with the same, 88
Bug arguing with a chicken, 115
Built like a brick outhouse, 114
Bull, 15-16, 43, 114
Bull calves, 90-91
Bull Durham, 23, 89
Bullfrogs, raining, 113
Bumpers rust, watching the, 84

129

Burn down the high school, 93
Bush, rag on the, 59
Busy, 29, 64-65
Butterick pattern dress, 56
Button(s), 17, 35, 98

Cabbage, cow ate the, 15
Cain, 88
Cajun, vii, 96
Calf/calves, 6, 10, 13, 90-91
Calf rope!, 10
California house, 26
Call(ed/ing), 31, 39
Calls to animals, 17
Calluses, 105-106
Carpet, 38, 39, 47
Carroll, Lewis, 78
Cassidy, Frederic, 25, 106
Cat(s), 27, 29, 84, 108, 115, 121
Catch barrel, 15
Catching 'em faster'n I can string 'em, 65
Chair(s), 2-3, 69, 121
Chaucer, Geoffrey, 33, 80
Chestnut, 120
Chicken(s), 8-9, 65, 75, 79, 92, 115
Chic sales, 26, 27, 98
Child, passion/sidehill, 55-56
Childhood, 70
Chin-lickin good, 84
Chin music, 45
Chips are down, 40
Chittlin, vii, 42
Chloe, drunk as, 33
Christmas, 15, 22-23, 60, 102
Chunk floater, 112-113
Church, 115, 121
Church is out, 63, 68-69
Churn, 65, 76, 85
Clarksville, Texas, 25, 82-83
Clean your plow, 14
Clear the topwaters!, 23-24
Clutch is slippin', 16-17
Co, boss!, 17
Coal, prairie, 9
Buckleburs, 43
Cockroach in a hot skillet, 115
Cold day in July, 94

Cold supper, spread out like a, 52
Colt, wood's, 56
C'mere from sic'im, 17, 92
Come in out of the rain, 92
Coming fresh, 68
Common as hens'/pig's tracks, 7
Cook naked for a deer camp, 42
Cooking on the front burner, 22, 106
Coon, 45, 94
Coon-ass, 96
Cooter Brown, 32-33
Cope!, 17
Cotton, 4, 15, 66-67, 70-71, 96
Cotton-eyed/headed, 70
Cottonseed for brains, 83
Country, so, 23, 49
Cow(s), 9, 15, 45, 78, 80, 113
Coyote, 96
Cracker, 96
Crap from wild honey, 92
Crapper, Thomas, 26
Crazy as a peach-orchard boar, 30
Crippled gelding, 32
Crockett, David, 41
Crooked as . . ., 114
Crop, planted their, 68
Crow, 119
Crowbar, tear up a, 43
Curlers, 47
Cut dog, 46
Cuts her teeth, 45

Dallas to Fort Worth!, 23-24
Dam buster, 113
Dance, 15
Dancing in . . ., 38
Dasher for her churn, 85
Day follow the night, 15-16
Dead and too dumb to fall over, 17
Dead man's hand, 24
Dear John, 69
Deck, full, 24
Democrat, 102
Demosthenes, 79
Dennis, Jim, 74
Deport, Texas, 83
Depot stove, 120

Devil, 78, 94, 101, 102
Dew, 27, 80
Dick's hatband, 101
Dickson, Paul, 33
Diddley squat, 92
Dingbat, 26
Dippers, 41
Dirt, 27-28, 30, 65, 94
Dishrag and all, 77
Dixie, whistling, 38, 115
Dobber, 27-28
Dog(s), 3, 5, 21, 29, 32, 37, 46, 52, 78, 79, 93, 102, 107, 114, 115, 116, 117, 121
Dog, hair of the, 44, 95
Dohan, Mary Helen, 69
Dollar knife, come close to the, 103
Donkey, pregnant, 121
Doo, 92, 93
Doohickey, 123
Doorknob, booger on a, 113
Doozie, 60-61
Dot an i, 93
Down in one's gitalongs, 122
Dressed up to the nines, 53
Drunkenness, 32-33, 119
Duck(s), 32, 79, 108, 113
Dugdale, R.I., 104
Dumb, 16-18, 92-93
Dyed in the wool, 102

Eagle's eye, 116
Ear, bat's, 116
Ear, pig's, 6
Ear, tin, 45
Earl, calling for, 31, 39
Eat a roastinear through a picket fence, 76
Eats supper before they say grace, 68
Eggs, 65, 117
Elevator, 16
Eleventh hour, 40
Enceinte, 68
Engaged, 59
Exciting as . . ., 84
Expecting, 68
Eye, eagle's, 116

Eyes bigger than stomach, 117

Faint heart, 24
Fair to middlin', 22
Falsie, 47
Family way, 68
Fare-thee-well, 14-15
Fast(er), 108
Fat, 22, 46, 52, 53
Fat lady sings, 52, 79
Fatted calf, 10
Fatwood, 81
Faulkner, William, 98, 117
Feather(ed/s), 52, 79, 88
Feet, 105-106
Fence, 68, 76, 83, 112-113
Ferris wheel, hub deep to a, 29
Fertilizer, sit on a sack of, 54
Fettucini Alfredo from stuffing, 92
Fiddle(r), 15, 33, 34
Fidity bag, 50
Fine as frogs' hair, 22
Fingers were made a'fore forks, 8
Fire, 3, 81, 120-121
First base, 92
First thing about, the, 92
Firstborn, mourneth for his, 123
Fish-flavored ice cream, 84
Fish market, tomcat in a, 84
Fish needs a bicycle, 32
Fish(ing), 27, 90
Fisk, Jim, 123
Fitter than a fat lady, 52
Flat-chested stripper, 115
Fleas, wake up with, 78
Flexner, Stuart, 89
Flock of guineas, 93
Floozie, 60
Flopped a lip over, 84
Fly dookie, 90
Fly in the buttermilk, 27
Fly's open, your, 70-71
Folk medicine, 9, 50
Foot, 105-106
Forest fire, 120-121
Four-button man, 98
Fox, 121
French lace, 47

131

Frot(s), 22, 112-113
Fruit won't fall far from the tree, 91
Frying of meat, 82
Full deck, not playing with, 24
Funeral, 43, 121
Funk, Charles Earl, 123
Futility, 90

Gabe's coat, 35
Garbage, eight acres of, 75
Gate off its hinges, 45
Gay deceiver, 47
Geein' when shouda been hawin', 6
Gentled, 54
Get hitched, 51
Gitalongs, 121-122
Give a dog a bad name, 21
Give a Rhett!, 34
Givey, 60
Gizmo, 123
Gnat's whisker, 116
Goat, 7-8, 26, 121
Gone to Texas, 98-99
Goners, 69
Good from bad, 92
Goose, 60, 93, 113
Gossip, 82-83
Got took down, 67
Got-up, 54
Got well, 107
Gourd vines, 87
Grand Canyon, 92
Grass widow, 55-56
Grasshopper in a henhouse, 32, 115
Gravy train, 83
Grease me!, 6
Greenville, 83
Grindstone, 78
Grinning like a jackass eating prickly pears, 78
Gritty as fish eggs, 84
Grose, Captain Francis, 33
GTT, 98-99
Guineas, flock of, 93
Gully washer, 113
Gussied up, 53-54

Hair in the butter, 27
Hair, let down her, 58
Hair of the dog, 44, 95
Half a bubble off plumb, 16
Half-wit, studying to be, 17
Haliburton, Thomas, 119
Haman, hung high as, 34
Hammers, sackful of, 118
Handy as . . ., 112
Hannah's hairbrush, hotter'n, 34
Happy as . . ., 84
Hard row to hoe, 67
Haricot, 4
Harrikin, vii, 3-4
Hat over the windmill, 57-58
Haul ass, 52
Haunt a house for fifteen cents, 42
Hay, 28, 55, 69-70
Hear himself think, 117
Hearthside metaphors, 81
Hector, 94
Hedge, 82
Heel(ed/s), 99, 105
Hefflefinger, Austin, 51
Heifer yearlings, raining, 113
Hell, 94, 120
Hen(s), 7, 15, 32, 52
Henry's old hoe, 34
Hesiod, 80
Hickey, 100
Hickman, Jim, 51
Hickok, Wild Bill, 24
Hickory switch, 18
Hide, 14, 15
Hidy, hi' you?, 22
High five, 109-109
High stepper, 43
Hill for a climber, 43
Hind leg, hold up, 31
Hind teat, 106-107
Hinges of hell, 120
Hip pocket(s), 30, 32, 112
Hitched, get, 51
Hitting the knots, 39
Hog(s), 4, 32, 37, 43, 79, 89, 96, 111, 115
Hog, blind, 43, 80
Hog, hip pockets on a, 32, 112

132

Hog, Hoover, vii, 34
Hog, root, or die, 79
Hog, wild, 60
Hog, wrestling, vii, 42
Homeopathy, 44
Homer, 78, 80
Hoodlum house, 26
Hoover . . ., vii, 34, 35
Horns off a billy goat, 45
Horse apples, 81-82, 113
Horsefeathers, 52
Horse manure, whitewashing, 90
Horseradish, 75
Horse, stick, 56
Horse turd as on a rose, 80
Hoss-high, 114
Hot as . . ., 120-121
Hound, 78
House, in the, 18-19
Howdied but ain't shook, 54
Hubbed it, 28-29
Humble pie, 89
Hunger, 7-8
Hydrophobia, 44

Ice cream, fish-flavored, 84
If I'm lyin' I'm dyin', 18
Ike-ing around, 34
Illegitimate, 55-56
I mean, 18
In the house, 18-19
Ink, brains was, 93
Irish pennant is flying, 71
It's time to . . ., 124

Jail, 79, 108-109
Jake's barn, 35
Jar, lid on the, 59
Jazz, 40
Jenkins, Dan, 16
Jeroboam, 33
Jessie, a goin', 35
Jewelry store, 23
Jingle of change, 82
Job's turkey, 91, 119
Johnson grass, 65
Juged, 105
Juke joint, 104-105

Jump the . . ., 6, 51
Jumper cables, 121
June bug, 29, 108
Junkyard dog, 46

Katie bar the door, 35
Kindlin', lay on a little more, 81
Kingsley, Charles, 78
Kitchen, 18-19
Knife, dollar, 103
Knitting bootees, 68
Knots, hitting the, 39

La!, 17
Labor, 95
Land, sorry, 55
Lardner, Ring, 76
Larrapin', 84
Last till the water gets hot, won't, 115
Latch on the outhouse door, 112
Lazarus, 29
Lazy as Uncle Deal, 60
Left field, out in, 16
Legs off a stove, 45
Lemonade, 52
Lick and a promise, 6
Lick by lick, the cow ate the grindstone, 78
Lick that calf again!, 6
Lick-log, 40-41
Lid on the jar, put the, 59
Lightbread, 89
Lighter wood, 81
Lightnin', greased, 108
Lightnin', white, 52, 96
Lights, 3-4
Lily, shake the dew off the, 27-28
Lip, flop a, 84
Lizard, 27-28, 29
Lloyd, David, 33
Load, two bricks shy of a, 16
Log(s), 39, 81, 113
Lopes and smokes, 106, 108
Lottie's eye, out like, 34
Love, a woman's, 80
Lower'n a mole's navel on digging day, 43

Luck, 83
Lumber room, 19
Lunch, ate his, 14-15

Man in the moon, 93
Manger, dog in a, 5
Marbles, 24
Mare's nest, 51-52
Mark of Cain, 88
Marry, 51-52
Marvell, 80
Mashed potato sandwich, 84
Mathews, Mitford, 40, 59, 119
Mean to shout, 18
Meat, frying of, 82
Mechanic, shade-tree, 30-31
Meetin' herself coming back, 65
Mel in jail, 35
Methodist(s), 41, 65
Mexican plate lunch, 75-76
Microwave cook-off, 121
Middlins, 89
Mighty big woman to weigh a ton, 58
Mink, 101
Minnow, 94
Minute, New York, 108
Mirror, sneak up on a, 42
Miss Claudie, lawdy, lawdy, 34
Miss Jones, 26
Miss Polly, good golly, 34
Missum, 57
Mithridates, 44
Miz Agnes, oh lawzy, 35
Miz-Astor rich, 34
Moby Dick, 94
Modest dog, 46
Mole's navel, 43
Money, made, 107
Monkey, brass, 45
Month of Sundays, 94
Moon, bark at the moon, 38, 80
Moonshine, 9, 52, 96
More'n one way to . . ., 78
Moseying, 69-70
Moss off your teeth, 76
Moulin Rouge, 58
Mountain dew, 96

Mountain oysters, 96
Mourneth for his firstborn, 123
Mouse, drunk as a, 33
Mule(s), 2, 6, 16, 43, 46, 71, 75, 117

Nails in the snow, 90
Navel, mole's, 43
Near-ox, 5
Nebuchadnezzar, 33
Neck as long as a well rope, 76
Negro, 113, 121
Nerd, 120
Nervous as . . ., 121
New York minute, 108
News, before God gets the, 108
Nightmare, hay for a, 28
Nina Ross, 34
Nine-rail fence, 2
Nines, to the, 53
Nitty-gritty, 40
Noisy as . . ., 117
Nonsense, 52
Nose, 76, 93
Nothin' from nothin', 93
Nut-cuttin', 40

Oar, just one in the water, 16
Oats, 76
Ofay, 118
Off-ox, 5
Older'n dirt, 94
One-armed/legged, 29
One-horse town, two buggies/carriages in a, 32, 43
One-syllable words, 112
Oprey ain't over, 79
O'Reilly's balls, 101
Ornery, 7
Outhouse, 27, 83, 112, 114
Outside child, 56
Oven, bakin' a cake in her, 68
Owls, tree full of, 84
Ox, 5-6, 27, 32, 51, 52, 119
Oysters, mountain, 96

Pacemaker at a microwave cookoff, 121
Paint to dry, waiting for the, 84

134

Pallet, Baptist, 65-66
Paper on the wall, 101
Paperhanger, one-armed, 29
Paris, Texas, vii, 51
Parlor room, 19
Parson's nose, 3-4
Parton, Dolly, 15-16
Passion child, 56
Pea turkey doo, 21, 93
Peach orchard, 30, 36, 121
Peck shit with the chickens, 8
Peckerwood, 118
Pee, 17, 91
Pepper patch, 121
Pie, humble, 89
Pig(s), 6, 7, 16, 32, 39, 113
Pine trees from pineapples, 93
Piss(ed/ing), 3, 30, 32, 43, 67, 93, 97
Pissant, 32
Pistol, two-dollar, 120
Pitchforks and Negro babies, raining, 113
Plow, clean your, 14
Plowin' up snakes, 27
Plunder room, 18-19
Pockets, 32, 112
Poke, 96
Poker, 23-24, 63, 68-69, 123
Pool, 81
Poontang, 49
Poor, 28, 54, 56, 89, 90-91, 99, 119
Poor-mouth, 54
Pope, vii, 3-4, 15-16
Pope, Alexander, 91
Porch, chickens under, 8-9
Porphyry, 95
Possum, 32, 96
Post wears out before hole, 85
Posthole auger, 114
Pot of . . ., 120
Pot, put big, into little, 10, 73, 77-78
Pot to pee in, 91
Pound sand in a rat hole, 43
Prairie coal, 9
Prayers of the sanctified, 67, 83

Pregnant, 4, 39, 68, 120, 121
Pretty as . . ., 4, 66
Prior, Matthew, 33
Prostitute, 43, 96
Proud, too, 91
Pryor, Cactus, 66
Publilius Syrus, 79
Pulling the wrong pig's ear, 6
Pump into believin' it's the windmill, 45
Pup, speckled, 4
Purple, born to the, 94-95
Push comes to shove, 40

Quick as, 108

Rabbits, 80
Rabies, 44
Rag on the bush, 59
Railroad track, thirty miles of, 24
Rain, come in out of the, 92
Rainstorms, 76, 112-113
Raise . . ., 55
Rat hole, 43
Rats, sawmill, 29
Rattlesnake, 84, 92
Rawhide boot, 76
Read'em and weep, 69
Read the riot act, 15
Ready-rolls, 54
Religion, got, 67
Renoir, 58
Restless as, 115
Rhett, 34
Rich get richer and the poor get children, 91
Riddle, Don, 23
Riding on the rims, 28
Riot act, 15
Road, bad, 76
Roastinears, 76, 89
Rock and a hard place, 78
Rocker-bottom feet, 105
Rode hard and put up wet, 43
Romeo and Juliet, 101
Roosevelt, T., 79
Root hog or die, 79
Rope, 10, 112

135

Rose, 80, 83
Round-heeled, 105
Row, hard, 67
Rump-sprung Sundays, 31

Saddle home, I brung your, 69
Sadie, sorrier than, 34
Sale, Charles, 26
Sally, long-tall, 35
Sam Hill, what in, 35
San Jacinto Day, 9
Sandstorm, 96
Sandwich, mashed potato, 84
Saucered but ain't been blowed, 54
Saved, 67
Sawing logs, 39
Sawmill rats, 29
Say grace, 64-65, 68
Scalded cat/dog, 46, 108
School, talking out of, 14
Second settin', 17
Seven miles of bad road, 76
Sewing machine, 121
Shade of a posthole auger, 114
Shade-tree mechanic, 30-31
Shadow, 116
Shakespeare, 78
Shandygaff, 52
Shinny, 9
Shit from Shinola, 93
Shoes his own mule, 117
Shroud, hip pockets on a, 112
Shuck, light a, 3, 78
Sidehill child, 55-56
Sidesaddle, 32
Sideways, didn't have no, 52
Silver City, New Mexico, 106
Similia similibus curantur, 44
Simon, stupid as, 34
Singletree, 6
Sit down in a number-three tub, 52
Sit up with, 71-72
Six-pack, vii
Skeletons fornicating on a tin roof, 117
Skepticism, 58
Skillet, 89
Skunk, 97

Sliced bread, 112
Slick(er), 113
Slip is showing, 70-71
Slippery as an eel in a barrel of snot, 113
Slop, hog in, 37
Slopjar, 113
Smart as a tree full of owls, 84
Smelling like a rose, 83
Smokehouse, 29
Smokes, lopes and, 106
Smyth, Admiral W.H., 94
Snakes, barrel of, 113-114
Snoring, 39
Snow, 90
Snowing down south, 71
Snuff, 31, 122
Snuffing, 94-95
Sod soaker, 113
Sod widow, 56
Son of a bitch, 89
Son of a gun, 94
Soo, cow!, 17
Soon, 107
Sooner baby, 56
Sophocles, 79
Sorrier than . . ., 55
Sow, 33, 36, 46, 121
Sowbelly, 89
Spank(ed/ing), 14, 83
Sparking, 38
Speak softly and carry a big stick, 79
Spider, 89
Split-pea-soup from honey, 93
Spread out like a cold supper, 52
Spring, ain't, 79, 82
Springer, heavy, 68
Sprinklers, 41
Squattin' when you ought to be squawkin', 6
Squirrel, 1, 82
Stationery, bathroom, 96
Stick closet, 26
Stick-to-your-ribs food, 117
Stiff in the heels, 99
Stirring the fire with a sword, 27
Stoop comes to grunt, 40

Storked, 68
Stout, 75, 122
Strange, dip his wick in the, 27-28
Straw, called to, 39
Straw hat to a Christmas tree, 22-23, 102
Straws, carrying, 38
Stubborn as, 117
Stuffing, 92
Stump mover, 113
Stung by a serpent, 68
Stupidity, 92-93
Suck it all out of his thumb, 91
Sucking the hind teat, 106
Summer name, 99
Sun set between their house and town, 117-118
Sunday school, 8
Sundays, month of, 94
Sundays, rump-sprung, 31
Supper, 52, 68
Surrender, 10-11
Swap spit, 78
Sweat, 53
Sweetnin', 89
Sword, stirring the fire with a, 27
Syatt, Dick, 4

Tail, dog's, 79
Taken up with, 56
Talk, 45, 58, 102
Talk turkey, 119
Talking like a cotton gin, 67
Talking out of school, 14
Tan your hide, 14
Tank, 81
Tar/tarred, 88
Tarkington, Booth, 50
Tarpley, Fred, 109
Teat(s), 106, 115
Teeth, 45, 76
Terlingua, 9, 76
Thin, 57, 116
Third base, 16-17
Thompson, Jimmy, 83, 107
Thrashing, 88
Thrift, 121-122
Throckmorton firewood, 9

Thumb, he didn't suck it all out of his, 91
Tie the knot, 51
Tight as . . ., 101
Time of day, 93
Tin 45, 117
Tires so thin you can see the air in them, 28, 117
Tit in the wringer, 27
Toad strangler, 113
Toilet, euphemisms for, 26
Toilet paper, 96
Tol'able, 22
Tomcat, 84, 115
Ton, weigh a, 58
Tongue, 45
Took down, 67
Toothbrush, hen needs a, 32
Topwaters, 23
Toulouse-Lautrec, 58
Town dog, 46, 52
Town, one-horse, 32, 43
Traces, jump the, 6
Tripe, 89
Troop train, 43
Trouble, 27
Truth'll always out, 80
Truthfulness, 15-16
Turd in a punch bowl, 112
Turkey, 21, 91, 93, 119, 120
Turner, Allton, 106
Turnips, load of, 2
Twain, Mark, 71, 88, 98
Twelfth hour, 40
Two-button man, 98
Two-car funeral, 32
Two-dollar whore, 120

Ugly, 35, 42, 67
Umbrella, 32, 54
Uncle Deal, 60
Uniform, turn in your, 69
Up from down, 93
Up the spout, 123
Useless, 8, 32, 43, 112, 115

Vaccinated with a Victrola needle, 45

Vamos, 69
Veranda, 19
Vietnam, 49
Vines, 87
Voice, raise your, 55

Wagon, 2-3, 4, 69
Warm as worm dirt, 30
Warming up leftover snow, 90
Water bill, pay his, 26
Watermelon(s), 2, 68, 87
Water's not hot, 111
Waters, troubled, 27
Wear you out, 14
Webster, Noah, 5
Well, fall out of a, 83
Well, got, 107
Well-heeled, 99
Whangdoodle, 123
Wheelbarrow with rope handles, 30, 90
Which way's up, 93
Whiffletree, 5-6, 51
Whisker, gnat's, 116
Whiskey through the jailhouse door, 79
Whistling Dixie, 38, 115
White house on the hill, 26
White lightnin', 52, 96
Whitewash, 90, 91
Whoops and hollers, 106, 108
Whore, 120, 121

Wick, dip his, 27-28
Wilder, Roy, Jr., 35
Wilson, Logan, 83
Wind, knock a hole in the, 118
Windmill(s), 32, 45, 57-58
Window to throw it out of, 91
Window weight, 79
Wing(s), 9, 15, 45
Wood, 2, 81
Woodbine twines, gone where the, 123
Woodpecker, 118
Wood's colt, 55
Woods, far out in the, 1, 117
Woods' hog, 60
Wool, 92, 96, 102
Worm dirt, 30
Would I lie to you?, 15-16
Wrapped up too tight, ain't, 16
Wrong side of the blanket, 56
Wutzi, 17

X-Y-Z, 71

Yank a plank off the wall, 81
Yardstick, 116
Yearling, The, 8
Yellow-dog Democrat, 102
Yellow jacket in the outhouse, 27

Zeus, drunk as, 33
Zipper, use him for a, 116